THE LEGACY SPECTRUM

Passing Your Wealth With

Thought And Meaning

THE LEGACY SPECTRUM

Passing Your Wealth With

Thought And Meaning

MARK A. WEBER

Edited by Kathryn A. Bolinske

VSP VINTON STREET PRESS

This book is intended to provide general information about the topics included. It is sold with the explicit understanding that while Mark A. Weber is an attorney, neither he, his employer (SilverStone Group) nor the publisher is engaged by the reader to provide legal, accounting, financial, tax or any other type of expert assistance. If the reader requires assistance in any of these areas, he or she should seek the assistance and services of a competent professional.

The sole purpose of this book is to educate. The author and his affiliates assume no liability or responsibility to any person or entity with respect to any loss or damage caused, or alleged to be caused, directly or indirectly by the information contained in it.

If you choose not to be bound by the statements above, you may return this book to the publisher for a full refund (less handling charges).

Finally, the author makes liberal use of case studies and examples from his own practice. The names of individuals, companies and other identifying facts have been changed to protect the identities of those involved. Therefore, any resemblance to actual individuals is purely coincidental.

First Edition, Second Printing
© 2017 Mark A. Weber
All rights reserved.
Printed in the United States of America
ISBN: 978-0-9990907-0-1

For information contact:
Mark Weber
MarkWeber@TheLegacySpectrum.com or
11516 Miracle Hills Drive, Suite 100
Omaha, NE 68154

THE LEGACY SPECTRUM

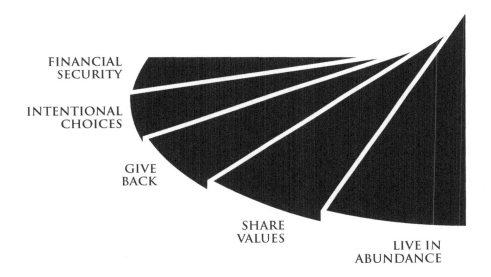

In The Legacy Spectrum you will learn to:

1. **Achieve** lasting financial security;

2. **Make** intentional choices about how much of an inheritance to leave;

3. **Give** back to the community in a meaningful manner;

4. **Share** personal values with your children in the process of teaching them to responsibly handle money; and

5. **Live** the last part of your life in abundance.

Rave Reviews For The Legacy Spectrum From Business Leaders, Parents And Advisors

Mark Weber's **The Legacy Spectrum** *is an essential guide when wrestling with questions about how much is "enough" for your lifetime security, what amount is "right" to help your heirs lead productive lives, and how much you might commit to creating a charitable legacy. With worksheets, case studies and commentary, Weber equips you to take charge of your decision-making process and get the best possible results.*

> Philip Cubeta, CLU®, ChFC®, MSFS, CAP®
> The Wallace Chair in Philanthropy
> The American College of Financial Services

Mark Weber's work to help families plan for transferring wealth and values is extraordinary in a number of ways. Mark encourages a shared clarity within families that leads to better decisions and better relationships. He helps us understand that a plan which includes values frees both parents and children from the bounds of money, and makes a better future possible for everyone involved – parents, children and community. Finally, the book confirms the idea that money, once accumulated, until shared, has no value.

> Mike McCarthy
> Chairman
> McCarthy Group LLC

The Legacy Spectrum *is EXTREMELY well written. It is written at the perfect level of depth with thought-provoking questions and believable family vignettes. I plan to have my wife and advisors read it and implement its teachings in our family's plans.*

> James T. Morris
> Chairman, President and Chief Executive Officer
> Pacific Life Insurance Company

Mark Weber is on the cutting edge of proactive philanthropy and has much to teach us all.

Jim Stovall
Best-selling Author, The Ultimate Gift

Mark Weber's book, The Legacy Spectrum should be required reading for advisors to high-net-worth clients. This is a must book for any thoughtful estate planner's toolbox.

Terence L. Horan
President / CEO
HORAN

Mark Weber's process for establishing a personal legacy when one exits this life draws from the same spring as I do for the process I recommend that owners use to establish their legacies when they exit their companies: personal values. In both, how we leave a legacy is important, but legacies are only successful if they are consistent with our goals and values. Estate planning can be so much more than passing property. In Weber's hands, it is.

John H. Brown
Founder of Business Enterprise Institute, Inc.
Author of Exit Planning: The Definitive Guide

The Legacy Spectrum…*is well written and will prove helpful to everyone who is confronted with the question, "What should I do with my estate?" The book is filled with ideas that will help anyone who hasn't yet made their final plans to give consideration to all the possibilities to benefit not only loved ones but their favorite causes that make their communities and the world a better place.*

William B. Wallace
Retired CEO
Phoenix Home Life Mutual Insurance Company

If more people of means read **The Legacy Spectrum**, *we would have more productive heirs and stronger communities!*

Mike Yanney
Chairman Emeritus
Burlington Capital

Legacy planning is among life's most meaningful exercises. But charting a course to make a lasting impact comes with challenges, including a deep exploration of your values, varied expectations, and difficult decisions. Mark's **Legacy Spectrum** *is an ideal resource for addressing these challenges, providing clarity that positions readers for sustainable success.*

Fred H. Jonske
President / CEO
M Financial Group

Mark Weber's **The Legacy Spectrum** *is a comprehensive, practical guide to navigating the complex waters of effective lifetime financial and legacy planning. The extensive use of case studies and examples are effective in marrying the "why" and "how" of a field that too often is focused upon minimizing taxes instead of maximizing impact. The book is a must read for both families developing legacy plans and to financial advisors providing counsel to those families.*

Robert R. Johnson, Ph.D., CFA, CAIA, CLF
President and CEO
The American College of Financial Services

The Legacy Spectrum *is not like any estate planning book out there because Weber incorporates the topics we really care about: legacy, values and family. The real-world examples Weber cites of families whose plans worked well (and not so well) are invaluable to those of us who are struggling to "do the right thing" with our own wealth planning.*

Ronald N. Quinn
Executive Vice President
Tenaska

The Legacy Spectrum *resonates on myriad levels, from providing an extremely pragmatic approach for determining how much to leave your children to providing an inspiring, thought-provoking rationale on the importance of leveraging your family bonds and financial assets to positively impact the community well beyond your lifetime. Weber's writing style is readily digestible. This is an incredibly important book – unlike any I've come across on this topic.*

Jeff Gordman
Former Chairman and CEO
Gordmans Stores, Inc.

We found Weber's book a perfect read at this time in our lives. It confirmed many of the actions we have been taking and offered several excellent ideas on how to improve our efforts.

Pete and Mary Anne Tulipana

For over 30 years I have worked for Creighton University as an attorney and gift planner. Like Weber, I've learned that donors are driven less by IRS deductions than they are by a desire to make a difference. **The Legacy Spectrum** *is a great read for anyone thinking about leaving a meaningful legacy to their children and charitable organizations they believe in. I'd also recommend it to any development officer who wants to give donors a practical tool in that decision-making process.*

Steven A. Scholer
Senior Philanthropic Advisor
Creighton University

Disposing of accumulated wealth thoughtfully is a daunting challenge. Otherwise decisive people can have trouble getting started. Weber's book provides a series of questions and actions to help overcome inertia so that people can develop a plan that is right for their families.

Wallace Weitz, CFA
Co-Chief Investment Officer, Portfolio Manger
Weitz Investments

This is a terrific book that I plan to share with current and prospective donors and recommend to colleagues in the charitable gift planning field.

Howard N. Epstein
Executive Director
Jewish Federation of Omaha Foundation

As a financial planner for nearly a decade, I've struggled with the legacy conversation with too many clients. **The Legacy Spectrum** *provides countless examples, stories and analogies that make this important conversation much easier. Weber's 30+ years of experience and wisdom are evident in the priceless stories and real-world case studies he provides throughout the book. A real page-turner and essential addition to any planner's library!*

Dan Kline
Senior Advisor, Financial Planning
First National Bank

Mark Weber has filled a vacuum in estate planning literature. Anyone thinking about generational wealth planning for their family should read this important book before making any final decisions. Mark's long personal and professional experience in Legacy Planning makes him very well qualified to explain how to go about what can sometimes seem to be a daunting process. I highly recommend this book.

Kelly O. Finnell
President/CEO
Executive Financial Services, Inc.

We've all benefitted in some way from those who came before us. In **The Legacy Spectrum**, *Mark Weber lays out a detailed blueprint for wealthy families intent on infusing future generations of family and community members with – not just wealth – but meaningful, life-enriching values.*

Steve Hill
Executive Director of Gift Planning
University of Nebraska Foundation

Weber identifies for both individuals and their advisors the key questions that need to be answered for any effective estate plan. With Weber's guidance individuals learn to leave not just an estate, but a legacy. Advisors learn to incorporate a client's answers into a truly meaningful plan.

> Nick R. Taylor
> Estate Planning Attorney
> Fitzgerald, Schorr, Barmettler
> & Brennan, P.C., L.L.O.

Weber does a great job of providing parents--both those who are new to and experienced in estate planning--tools and techniques, self-assessment questions, sample letters, and guides for more ideas on how to create a comprehensive estate plan. The transparency Weber recommends between parents and children will help both parents and children better understand the rationale for parents' estate planning decisions.

> A. William "Bill" Kernen
> President
> Kernen Capital, LLC

Great book for wealthy individuals who want to take their planning to the next level. **The Legacy Spectrum** *also provides a roadmap for advisors who want to take their practices to the next level and determine what motivates their clients.*

> Jeff Snyder
> Tax & Consulting Partner
> Lutz

The Legacy Spectrum *is a must read for parents and advisors alike. Author Mark Weber has personally gone through the planning process as a child with his parents, and as an adult with his own family. He has also advised hundreds of wealthy families. To have true life-stories available is invaluable. Great book.*

> Michael I. Silverberg, ChFC, CLU
> Managing Principal
> Lindberg & Ripple

This vital how-to reference, with worksheets, stories and examples, is a clear guide for wealthy families. It shows them how to intentionally and purposefully link together their wealth with their most important values and lessons so they can pass them on and give lasting meaning to that wealth for generations to come.

Jamie Worrell
Managing Partner
Strategic Retirement Partners

Mark does a masterful job in moving the focus of effective estate planning from a transactional, tax-driven event to a process whose foundation is built on value-based thinking designed to create a lasting legacy for families. He challenges and encourages families and their advisors to collaborate in getting at what really matters and to develop planning strategies to drive results in their pursuit. The book is full of case studies and real-world examples of how to put "Money and Values in Motion." Without a doubt families will get better results and enjoy greater peace of mind from their planning by using Mark's tools and techniques presented in **The Legacy Spectrum**.

Leonard M. Sommer, CPA
President
Hancock & Dana, PC

The Legacy Spectrum *gets to the real challenge of planning...what is it I really want for my family? My community? How can I truly make a difference?* **The Legacy Spectrum** *gives you a practical approach to discern your answers.*

Ernest Barry
Partner
Barry, Evans, Josephs & Snipes

The Legacy Spectrum *is a reflection of author Mark Weber's values as a person, a professional and a community leader. Mark's book provides a framework for helping people of significant means leave a legacy to their families and communities in a thoughtful and considerate way. I believe it will be transformative to the planning industry.*

Thomas J. Scalici
Chief Executive Officer
Cornerstone Advisors Asset Management, LLC

If you have been fortunate enough to accumulate more wealth than you can spend, then you must read **The Legacy Spectrum***! It will guide you, with loving care, through all the decisions that you should be considering. After fifty years in and around finance I have never seen a better, clearer or more thoughtful guidebook to help you build your legacy. Splendid work, Weber!!*

L. B. "Red" Thomas
Retired Vice President
ConAgra, Inc.

Table of Contents

Dedication

I dedicate this book to my wife, siblings and children.

Tricia is my soulmate of 42 years, best friend and mother to our five children and nine grandchildren. She steadfastly encouraged me during the many evenings and weekends spent writing alone in my home office. She is my voice of reason.

My first experience of running family meetings was organizing, conducting and acting on decisions made during meetings with my parents and seven siblings. From them I learned how each individual brings an important dynamic that makes a family unique. Over the 15 years that we met, I felt our love and respect for each other increase. The bonds we built in those meetings helped keep us emotionally close years after our parents' deaths. I thank each of my siblings (Nancy, Paul, Phil, Kathleen, Chuck, Jim and Russ) for their patience and lessons.

Many of the concepts I share in this book I have tested on my own family. My five children (Nathan, Nicky, Jackie, Megan and Jill) have been "guinea pigs" of sorts for our family's meetings and philanthropy. I thank them for their faith in me, and their openness to new ideas— even those that didn't work out so well!

In addition to the legacy my wife and I are creating for our children, I wish to leave a professional legacy to advisors. I want more of them to help individuals create legacies that intentionally pass both wealth and values to their children, prepare those children to receive wealth and, through philanthropy, bring families closer together and improve communities. For that reason, I am donating all of the profits from the sale of this book to the Charitable Advisor in Philanthropy Program.

Is This Book For You?

It is if you are an individual who:
1. Has accumulated enough wealth for your own financial security. In other words, you will not consume all of your assets during your lifetime.

2. Is committed (whether you have children or not) to being intentional with your financial surplus.

3. Desires to leave behind a legacy in the form of:

   · Passing your values--along with money--to your children; and

   · Making your community a better place to live.

4. Has passed through the first two phases of financial life, (namely *accumulation* and *preservation*) and, having moved into the *distribution* phase, is focused on estate planning.

5. Is willing to dedicate time, thought and resources to the design and implementation of a plan that will help draw your family closer together during and after your lifetime.

It is if you are a professional advisor who:
1. Works with affluent individuals.

2. Enjoys developing strong personal relationships with your clients.

3. Is committed to building stronger families and communities.

4. Works well with other professionals to reach a common goal.

Introduction

I wrote this book for a relatively small, but financially sophisticated and influential audience. For that reason, I will focus on the questions and issues that matter most to them and avoid the topics that don't.

Questions That Matter

· How do you know how much is enough for your financial security?

· How much money should you leave your children?

· How do you use your money to help your children (and/or grandchildren) become responsible adults and good community citizens?

· How do you give back to the community that has given you so much?

· How do you get the most out of your advisors?

· How can you be confident that your plan will achieve your goals should you lose physical or mental capacity?

Topics That Don't

While taxation is an important aspect of estate planning, I have intentionally avoided discussing the technicalities of tax planning whenever possible. Instead, I ask you to reflect on broader, personal issues dealing with family and values. These questions go to the heart of meaningful planning. Your professional advisors can address topics such as taxes, trusts, investments etc.

Organization

You need not read this book from beginning to end to gain valuable insight. I encourage you to read the chapters that are most pertinent to your situation. The chapter titles are designed to help you easily identify the topics you may find of greatest interest.

I've limited the information in each chapter to the most important points and have used the Appendix for worksheets and letters. There is also a list of resources should you want more detailed information on a specific topic.

The Legacy Spectrum

There is a broad spectrum of actions you can take to leave the legacy you want. Many individuals, however, and for that matter, many estate planning professionals, have never considered the legacy planning process in terms of points along a continuum. For example, if you don't really care what happens to your assets after you die, you are at the left end of the spectrum. If you wish to pass financial assets with as little tax liability as possible, you are closer to the middle. If, however, you want to equip your children with the skills necessary to manage wealth, give generously and work well together as a family, you are near the right end of the spectrum.

At the end of each chapter, you will find a list that describes each point on a continuum of actions you can take in planning your legacy. The actions are not judgmental or prescriptive. They simply indicate possible actions and those others have taken in their legacy planning.

While we are all individuals and our family situations vary, each of us who wishes to leave a legacy must address three universal questions:

· How much is "enough" to assure my financial security?

· How much is "enough," but not too much, for my children?

· How do I leave a legacy to my children and community?

For simplicity, the Legacy Spectrum for each of these three questions relates to the most common situation: a married couple with shared biological or adopted children. However, every family is unique. Your answer to each question may vary based on your specific situation. For example, you may be single, divorced or remarried, have special needs children or children experiencing addiction, etc. Regardless of the specifics of your family, you must still answer the three questions above to determine your legacy.

I encourage you to locate your current location on the spectrum. If you are married, I encourage each spouse to do so. The differences in opinion can be surprising, but must be negotiated before bringing children into any discussion of inheritance.

If you can achieve the goals you set for your legacy at the point on the spectrum where you are today, great! If the actions you've taken so far do not accomplish your financial and personal goals, you may wish to incorporate some of the techniques you will find in this book.

In the end, the purpose of each spectrum is to show you that planning for the successful disposition of your assets is possible but may require more action on your part.

What are people like you doing about their legacies?

I've collected numerous stories about legacy planning from my work with wealthy individuals as well as from the guest speakers who have addressed our CAP® Study Group over the past six years. These speakers are in the top one percent of wealth holders in our country, and each has a fascinating life story. Each of them has thoughtfully planned to include philanthropy and pass personal values to the next generation in their estate plans.

All of them have grappled with and addressed the issues that I suggest you tackle in this book: how much is "enough" for themselves, how much they should leave their children and how to leave a meaningful legacy to their families and communities after they are gone.

You may wonder, as I did when I first invited highly successful individuals to address our group, why they would share their deeply personal stories with strangers. Estate plans are highly confidential and these are very private people. It soon became apparent that they had devoted many hours, and often years, to fine tuning and implementing their estate plans. They were willing to share what had worked (and not worked) for their families as another way of giving back to the community. They understood that if they could inspire even one advisor who in turn inspired his or her clients to give more responsibly to their children and community, they could leverage their efforts to create a better world.

To protect the confidentiality of every individual whose story I tell, I do not use actual names or fact patterns. I do, however, share enough information to answer the question we all ask, "What do other people like me do?" It is my hope that these stories will inspire you when you are creating a legacy plan designed to build a stronger family, pass on your values and improve the community in which you live with the confidence that you are making a difference in this world.

Author's Notes

Give me a lever long enough and a fulcrum
on which to place it and I shall move the world.
ARCHIMEDES

"I challenge you to make our community the most generous community per capita in the country!" Standing just 15 feet away, Warren Buffett seemed to be talking directly to me as he addressed that night's gathering of philanthropists. He continued, "Are you doing everything you can to make our community number one in giving?" His challenge rang in my ears that night and for the next couple of weeks when I decided to accept it.

Buffett issued that challenge over six years ago at a United Way dinner and it continues to inspire me today in my work with affluent families and in my role as a spouse and parent to five grown children. Ultimately, his challenge is the inspiration and goal for this book: I hope that what I share here will: 1) inspire you to leave a legacy to your children and community that will make them better and 2) give meaning to your lifetime of hard work.

I know that wealthy individuals rarely make significant charitable gifts without the advice and counsel of their professional advisors because I am one of those advisors. I have a law degree, a master's degree in financial services and several industry professional designations. In these disciplines, we tend to focus on the *tax aspects* of transferring assets, not the *legacy aspects*. That's entirely understandable because neither law schools nor business schools teach students to help individuals identify the legacies, both financial and personal, that they wish to leave upon their deaths.

Reaching professional advisors, I realized, was my key to meeting Mr. Buffett's challenge. Teaching professional advisors that there is so much more to leaving a legacy than simply avoiding taxes was my initial goal. The question was, how?

The platform I chose was the Omaha Community Foundation. Since its mission includes "promoting philanthropy throughout the community," I proposed that it host study groups of professional advisors. I believed that we could learn to ask our clients (individuals who were creating their estate plans) questions that would elicit their values, dreams and goals. If we actively listened to their responses, we could help individuals leave legacies that would benefit their families and communities and attach meaning to the financial assets they had worked to accumulate. I chose, as a basis, the curriculum for the accredited Chartered Advisor in Philanthropy (CAP®) program from The American College for Financial Services.

I suggested that we invite a dozen local professional advisors to form the first study group. Simultaneously, members of the group would take the CAP® program's online classes and supplement those classes with 15 two-hour meetings. I would facilitate those meetings during which one speaker (or a panel) would make a presentation followed by candid discussion. The Foundation's leadership saw the potential and readily agreed.

Five years later we have over 60 CAP® graduates in the Omaha area. This year, we will graduate a dozen more. Today there are over 20 new study groups based on the CAP® Study Group Model in communities across the United States. Increasingly, estate planning professionals are able to help individuals discover and create their legacies in greater numbers than ever before. In Omaha we are meeting Mr. Buffett's challenge one conversation at a time between philanthropically inclined individuals and advisors.

What is a Personal Legacy or Legacy Planning?

We typically think of our legacies as the lump sum of financial assets that we leave, at our deaths, to the people or organizations we choose. I consider that estate planning. Traditional estate planning does a good job of passing financial assets tax efficiently. Unfortunately, it also does an equally good job of passing wealth *free from the values of those who are doing the passing!*

The legacy you leave can be so much more than financial assets. Your legacy can include teaching your children to become productive, contributing citizens and to manage wealth responsibly. It can include providing your children the tools they will need to get along with each other as adults, make difficult family decisions, contribute to their communities and pass on your values to their children. Legacy planning then, is the work that you (and your advisors) do to distribute *both your financial assets and values.*

Incorporating values about spending, saving, investing and giving away wealth is a broader way to view your legacy. The process of intentionally passing both financial assets and your values surrounding those assets to your children can give your life meaning and build stronger families and communities.

What's The Problem?

From the time our children are toddlers and throughout their school years, we teach them our values: kindness, respecting others, honesty, playing by the rules, hard work, etc. We teach them very little about money and share little (or none) of our feelings about it. Only when we die and they receive our assets do most of our children learn how much money we've left them. And that manual that tells them how we want them to use the money we've left? There isn't one.

Why, then, are we so surprised when our children are incapable of managing large sums of money? Similarly, why are we disappointed when our children fight over our money when we never taught them to work together toward a common goal?

What I Hope To Contribute

There are many excellent articles and books written on the various aspects of legacy planning and I've read many of them. In writing this book, I have synthesized what I've read with the best practices from three additional sources:

1. Thirty years of experience working with wealthy individuals,
2. Materials from the Chartered Advisor in Philanthropy® curriculum, and
3. The life experiences and insights shared by some of the presenters to our CAP® Study Group.

From all of these sources, I offer the following insights:

· Signing your estate planning documents is not the end of the planning process. It is only one step, and I'd argue just a first step, on a spectrum of actions you can take to prepare your children to inherit wealth responsibly.

- Determining the appropriate amount to leave your children and teaching them how to use their inheritance responsibly are not tasks you can delegate. You must accept this responsibility and effectively communicate your wishes to your advisors.

- You can't do this alone. To live the final phase of your life with confidence that you will not outlive your resources and develop an effective legacy plan requires your own personal board of advisors. I'm confident that you have the resources in your community to do both if you take the initiative to tell your advisors that you want more than a traditional estate plan.

I include insights into what some of America's wealthiest individuals are doing to pass on their values along with their money to their children to inspire you to do the same.

If you have significant financial assets, it is my hope that you will incorporate legacy planning into your estate plan. If you are an advisor, I hope this book will help you offer broader, more meaningful counsel to your clients. No matter who you are I challenge you to think beyond passing simply monetary wealth.

Leaving a legacy then is a journey; one in which you set the terms. As you begin yours, I wish you the best. Enjoy it. The joy is in the journey.

Where Do You Begin?

Legacy planning is an ongoing process rather than a one-time thing. It takes initiative and effort on your part but the benefits to you, your children, your family as a whole and your community are enormous. I encourage you to incorporate your values into your legacy. Your role as your children's teacher doesn't end when your children finish school. If you didn't teach your children about your values surrounding money from the time they are young, it is never too late to begin.

CHAPTER 1

Money And Values In Motion

It is the heart that makes a man rich. He is rich according to what he is, not according to what he has.
HENRY WARD BEECHER

We are one of the wealthiest nations in the world, and as a country, we are in the process of transferring the greatest amount of wealth in our history. Individuals in the "second half" of their lives are driving this transfer, and many of them want to transfer their values along with their money to the next generation.

Traditional estate planning helps us pass our wealth with little or no federal estate taxes, but estate planning is not legacy planning. Estate planning does little, if anything, to help us pass our values to our heirs, nor does it prepare our heirs to receive significant inheritances.

In the first half of life, we raise our children and work to instill our values in them. Once they finish their formal education and leave our homes, we assume our job as parents is complete. We give them little practical financial education and the first time they learn about our finances is when they read our wills in an attorney's office after our deaths.

Yet we are surprised when children are unprepared to handle a sudden large inheritance and that families fracture in fights over parents' money.

There is an alternative to unprepared children and broken families. Legacy planning is designed to prepare your children to manage wealth responsibly so is a supplement to traditional estate planning.

Your estate plan is a stack of legal documents. Your legacy plan is a process that uses estate planning as a springboard. You choose the goals you want to accomplish for yourself, your family and your community.

Legacy Planning Raises The Bar

I will share the personal stories of some families who have moved beyond traditional estate planning. In choosing to pass on values as well as wealth, these individuals have done more than sign documents. They have found great meaning in preparing their heirs to receive wealth by actively transferring their family values through purposeful interaction.

Through legacy planning, you too can:

1. Live your remaining years free of financial fear.
2. Enrich your relationship with your children.
3. Teach your children to use their inheritance in accordance with your values.
4. Nurture your soul by giving back to your community and inspiring your children to do the same.
5. Discover how to maximize the value of your professional advisors.

WHO'S GOT THE MONEY?

Experts project that over $100 trillion will change hands in the coming decades as the older generations die and pass wealth to their children. It is helpful to understand how generations are divided and which ones currently hold the wealth.

· If you were born before 1945, you are part of the "World War II," or "Silent Generation."

· If you were born between 1946 and 1964, you are a "Baby Boomer."

· If you were born between 1965 and 1980, you are a "GenXer."

· If you were born between 1980 and the early 1990s, you are a "Millennial."

· The "Next Gen" often refers to the combined generations of "GenXers" and "Millennials."

In the following pages, I'm going to ask you several questions about wealth; questions that I think will help you and your spouse lay the groundwork for the decisions you'll make about your own wealth.

Question 1. Who do you think owns most of the wealth in the United States?

Despite all the publicity surrounding young Silicon Valley tech billionaires, Baby Boomers and their parents control over three quarters of the wealth in America! That's why I've written this book for the "seventy-five percent."

Question 2. How important is it to you to leave an inheritance?

Most of us wish to leave money to our children, but few of us can articulate exactly why. As a result, our attorneys draft estate plans that pass as much money as possible to our children. My purpose in asking this question is not to judge whether doing so is a good or bad thing. Rather, my purpose is to prompt you to consider why you desire to leave an inheritance before you determine how large it should be.

Have you and your spouse had a frank conversation about why each of you wishes to leave money to your children? If you have, have you discussed how much money you wish to leave them? Are you both in agreement? Or does one of you want to leave this world broke while the other feels an obligation to leave a big chunk of cash to your children?

The key is to openly discuss these questions with each other and come to a consensus. Finally, you must clearly communicate your wishes to your professional advisors.

Question 3. If you decide to leave an inheritance, how confident are you that your heirs can handle what you leave?

In my experience, it is common for parents to be concerned about the detrimental effect that a large inheritance might have on their children. This is particularly true for grandparents who contemplate leaving money to grandchildren.

There is one group of parents, however, that often does not share this concern: parents who have worked, usually for years, with their children in family businesses. First, these parents have had the opportunity to mentor their children and watch their children make increasingly important business/financial decisions. Second, the assets these parents are passing are in the form of inventory, equipment, real estate and goodwill. Parents who own family businesses generally express far more confidence in their children's ability to handle an inheritance than do parents who contemplate passing cash or other liquid assets.

It is common for parents to be concerned about the detrimental effect that a large inheritance might have on their children.

Newspapers and online news sources are full of stories about celebrities, athletes and lottery winners who destroy their families and their lives after suddenly coming into too much money when they are unprepared to manage it. Many of us can tell our own stories of friends, neighbors, acquaintances or clients who were unprepared for sudden wealth and fall prey to predators, financial hucksters and exotic investment schemes. Many are broke in a just few years. Others, addicted to easy money, never achieved their true potential.

Ironically, many parents leave their children significant inheritances with the very best intentions. They want their children to sidestep some of the hardships they experienced on their paths to financial success. They believe that the best way to smooth their child's path is cash: multiple and large gifts of cash. In this belief, they remind me of the story of the man and the cocoon.

One day a man found a butterfly cocoon with a small opening. He sat and watched for hours as the tiny butterfly struggled to force its body through that little hole. Then the butterfly stopped making progress. It appeared as if it could go no further.

So the man decided to help the butterfly. With a pair of scissors, he snipped off the remaining bit of the cocoon. The butterfly then emerged easily, but it had a swollen body and small, shriveled wings.

The man continued to watch the butterfly because he expected that, at any moment, its wings would enlarge and expand and its swollen body would contract.

Neither happened! In fact, the butterfly spent the rest of its short life crawling on the ground with a swollen body and shriveled wings. It never was able to fly.

What the man, in his kindness and haste, did not understand was that the restricting cocoon forced the butterfly to struggle to get through the tiny opening. This design was God's way of forcing the fluid from the body of the butterfly into its wings so that the butterfly could fly once it freed itself from the cocoon.

Sometimes struggles are exactly what we need to be successful in our lives. If God allowed us to go through our lives without any obstacles, we would never reach our full potential. We would not be as strong as we are after overcoming challenges. Without struggle we cannot fly!

The desire to protect our children is a good thing when they are young. As they age, however, if we become helicopter parents and don't give children the tools to overcome challenges and "rescue" themselves, we rob them of the possibility of becoming independent, confident adults.

Our current system of estate planning does nothing to help parents teach children to manage the wealth they will receive. Nor does it adequately tackle the other issue that the owners of our country's wealth are most concerned about: Passing on values and life lessons.

Question 4: What do you feel is the most important inheritance you can pass to your heirs?

Answering this question can take some soul-searching and candid, heart-felt conversation between spouses. A person's will and trust deal with financial assets. Surprisingly, or perhaps not, wealthy families tell researchers that money is one of the least important "assets" they plan to leave to their children. Topping the list are values and life lessons.

To understand why our current estate planning process is simply not conducive to passing parental values and lessons to children, nor equipping children to responsibly manage large financial inheritances, let's look at how estate planning is usually approached.

How Most Of Us Approach Estate Planning

Virtually no one looks forward with excitement to doing their estate planning. Rather, with a sense of obligation to our children and duty to "plan" for our deaths, we move in that direction. If not motivated by obligation, the death of someone close to us prompts us to make the call. While we want to make certain that we provide for those we love, there is little appeal in facing our own mortality and giving away assets we've spent a lifetime accumulating.

Prior to our first meeting with our attorney, spouses typically spend precious little time answering the questions I've asked here, much less discussing, clarifying and prioritizing their goals. Pre-meeting conversations usually begin and end with, "I want to make certain you are financially secure. After you die, the kids can have whatever money is left. Do you want to meet me at the attorney's or will we go together?"

We give no thought to:

1. The values we, as parents, want to pass on to our children,

2. How we want our children to use the money we leave,

3. Whether an inheritance will have a constructive or destructive effect on our children, and

4. How we might use a portion of our wealth to express our gratitude for all that we've received.

Certainly, we don't commit much time, if any, to considering how the estate planning actions we are about to take might bring our families closer together and provide us an opportunity to educate our children.

With no information about:

1. How important passing an inheritance is to you,

2. How you want your children to use that inheritance,

3. Whether there are values and lessons you'd like to pass to children along with your assets, and

4. Whether you have any interest (assuming that there is money to do so) in including charitable causes in your legacy,

estate planning attorneys are left to make their own assumptions. They rely on their training and the judgment they've developed over years to create wills and trusts that pass financial assets to heirs in a way that protects as much of that amount as possible from taxation.

Take The Initiative

In the chapters that follow you will learn that creating a Legacy Plan—a plan that passes your values and financial assets to your heirs in a way that not only brings you closer as a family, but also

- **Communicates** your values about money to your children,

- **Gives** your children the tools they need to use the assets you leave wisely, and

- **Attaches** meaning to your financial assets as you use them to give back to your community,

– only happens if you take the initiative. You must set the course and communicate your goals to your advisors.

I've created worksheets to help you and your spouse do exactly that. (See the Appendix or visit *www.TheLegacySpectrum.com* to download them.) Worksheets will spark conversation and help you define the type and size of inheritance most appropriate for your family. Only when you and your spouse have gained agreement and clarity about your goals can you articulate them to your advisors. Armed with that information, your advisors can pick up the ball and create a plan, a Legacy Plan, that carries out your wishes.

You can do this. I know because most of the people whose stories appear in this book all started where you are: they all had worked with experienced, highly skilled estate planning attorneys to pass financial assets to their children, but most wanted to pass values as well. In the end, the "estate plans" that they created evolved into Legacy Plans because they worked with their advisors to do more than accomplish tax-advantaged distributions of their assets.

The Stakes Are High

There is no room in traditional estate planning for preparing children to responsibly handle a large inheritance. Nor do traditional estate plans do a good job of passing on our values and life lessons to our children.

If we continue to do estate planning in the "traditional" way, we will continue to get the same results. We can do better.

In the midst of this historic transfer of wealth in our country, it is up to each of us to accept some responsibility to ensure that our share of that wealth is wisely used after our deaths. By incorporating legacy planning into our traditional estate planning, we accept that responsibility and, in doing so, positively impact our families and communities.

There is no room in traditional estate planning for preparing children to responsibly handle a large inheritance.

CHAPTER 2

How Much Is Enough?

Abundance is not a number or acquisition.
It is the simple recognition of enoughness.
ALAN COHEN

Before we can do any meaningful estate planning, it is essential that we are confident that we will have financial security in our later years. We will not make significant lifetime gifts to our children, much less our communities, if we fret over whether we will have enough for ourselves.

Few people know how to achieve that confidence, erroneously thinking that greater net worth automatically assures financial security. This chapter provides a roadmap to take you from where you are today to being confident that you have "enough." It also outlines how you can maintain that confidence for the rest of your life.

DETERMINING HOW MUCH IS "ENOUGH" FOR YOU

We spend our working careers, often 40 to 50 years or more, generating enough money to support ourselves during both our working and retirement years. Once income from our labor stops and we are dependent on investment earnings, it can be disconcerting.

It is quite common and natural to wonder about:

- **What if** my spouse suddenly dies?

- **What if** we have a medical emergency?

- **What if** one (or both) of us gets Alzheimer's?

- **What if** one or both of us has to go into a nursing home?

· **What if** one of our children gets divorced and/or needs significant financial help?

· *What if...?*

All of these events are financial stressors and thinking about how they can affect your life is a natural and necessary step toward confidence in having "enough."

What's Your Retirement Number?

An insurance company television commercial pushing the sale of retirement saving products took a clever approach to calculating "enough." An actor posits the question, "What is your number?" The camera follows people involved in daily activities while carrying placards of their "number," (e.g. $3,643,201 or $5,127,989, etc.).

It is a clever commercial and effectively makes the point that we should calculate how much money we must accumulate to generate enough income during retirement to replace the incomes we enjoyed during our working years. In reality, however, the equation is more complex than punching some numbers into a calculator to get the answer. The number or dollar amount that gives you confidence in your ability to live comfortably throughout your retirement years is the result of a multi-faceted process that takes some time and requires help from financial professionals.

Not only is the calculation more complicated than advertised, we have been deluded into believing that retirement is a destination. If we build a big enough pile of chips at retirement, we are home free! We will live a worry-free life, sipping cold drinks on a warm beach in paradise.

But retirement doesn't work that way. Retirement is not a point in time, but another phase of our lives. If we are worriers now, we will worry then.

The stressors mentioned in this chapter never really go away. Often anxiety gets worse as we age. Unfortunately, I see too many people who can never be comfortable that they have "enough."

BUILDING YOUR ROADMAP TO CONFIDENCE: STEP BY STEP

The very first step in answering, "How much is enough to assure my financial security?" is to capture a clear picture of the amount of cash you currently spend. The second step is to use that snapshot of current spending to anticipate how much you will need when the paychecks stop.

Step One: Establish A Current Budget

I am constantly amazed by how few people develop and maintain a household budget. By "budget," I do not mean recording every dollar you spend on an electronic spreadsheet, although doing so is excellent discipline when you first establish a household!

I'm talking about having a clear understanding of how much spendable income you need to maintain your current lifestyle. You can calculate this income amount yourself by reviewing your checkbook and credit card bills for the last couple of years. Alternatively, you can hire your accounting firm to do it for you. Ask your advisors to review it so they can help you build in a cushion for items you've forgotten, and establish a fund for unforeseen emergencies. Whether you collect the data yourself or have your accountant do so, you need to be comfortable with the ultimate result.

Step Two: Anticipate Future Income And Expenses

Your current budget is the platform for estimating the amount of cash you'll need during your retirement years. As you and your advisors calculate that number, you will answer a multitude of questions:

- What income will I receive (from, for example, Social Security, pension, 401(k), deferred compensation, interest and dividends)?
- Will certain expenses decrease? These might include 401(k) contributions, private medical insurance, disability insurance premiums and payroll deductions.
- Will certain expenses increase such as travel or those associated with a second home?
- What inflation rate is reasonable to expect?
- What is a reasonable rate of return to expect?

· What will my income taxes likely be?

· What is my realistic life expectancy and that of my spouse?

· When should I start to take Social Security benefits?

· Which assets should I spend first?

There are sophisticated software programs that, with help from a skilled retirement planner, can help you model various answers to these questions.

Step Three: Stress Test Your Future Budget

It is completely natural to have lingering doubts about our well-planned budgets. We can think of a million things that might torpedo them. For example, if the stock market takes a nosedive, if we run up major medical bills, or if our children need help, how will our budget be affected?

The simple act of making a written list of your questions and concerns can be cathartic. It exposes subliminal, unnamed fears to the light of day. From this perspective you can examine, discuss and address them. Your list of questions and concerns will change over time as you and the world around you changes. What is important is to continually acknowledge our fears to ourselves and to our advisors.

It's been my experience that we are best off using a retirement planning specialist to help us navigate the retirement planning process. They have the software, they know how to use it and they've helped many other people to run the numbers.

Step Four: Assess Your Emotional State

In addition to the math calculations necessary to create your Roadmap To Confidence, there are psychological or emotional factors to consider. As we age and move further from the workplace, it is natural to feel more financially vulnerable. Similarly, as our bodies age, we find ourselves increasingly dependent on others. We can become fearful of an environment and aging process over which we have less and less influence.

Some fear is healthy: it makes us pay attention to the accuracy and breadth of our calculation process. Comprehensive calculations give many, but not all, of us confidence in the numbers they yield. For all of us, there's an emotional component to our "enough" number, but some can be so paralyzed by fear that no amount of money, no matter how carefully calculated is ever "enough."

To illustrate that having "enough" is not solely an objective, mathematical calculation, I share a few stories.

The Paralysis of Fear

A client once asked me to help his father ("George") update his estate plan. George was about 85-years old and had sold a very successful, third-generation business ten years before. Almost all of his nest egg of $50,000,000 was in bank accounts and the stock market. George and his wife ("Mildred") lived frugally and spent between $100,000 to $120,000 on living expenses per year. George reinvested virtually all of his investment earnings.

George and Mildred had simple wills leaving all of their assets to each other and whatever was left, equally to their children. George's primary estate planning goals were: 1) financial security for Mildred and himself, and 2) leave as much as they could to their adult children. I pointed out to George that since his investment earnings alone exceeded $1,000,000 annually, he had more money than he could ever spend.

I suggested that, in order to meet his goals, George and Mildred begin making lifetime gifts to their children and grandchildren to reduce the size of their taxable estate and shift future appreciation of assets to their children.

George rejected my suggestions. He explained that he had lived through the Great Depression, saw the stock market crash, banks fail and his parents lose everything. Despite being a multimillionaire, George never felt he had "enough."

This fear froze both George and Mildred into inaction. As a result of their unwillingness to make transfers to their children during their lifetimes, the estate paid nearly $20,000,000 in estate taxes. Had George and Mildred been able to overcome their fears of not having "enough," much of the $20,000,000 *could have been directed to their children, grandchildren and/ or the charities they cared about.*

By any objective measure, George and Mildred had more than enough money to retire free of worry. Yet they feared the worst until the very end.

I am not making light of George and Mildred's fears. They had reason to be scarred as they witnessed their parents struggle. Consider the following:

· In 1933, the unemployment rate was 25 percent.

· While no agency kept track of foreclosure rates, reports of the Federal Home Loan Board showed 1,000 home loans per day placed into foreclosure.[1]

· Average family income fell (on average) 40% between 1929 and 1933.

While we cannot control much of what happens to us throughout our lives, we can control how we react to each challenge thrown our way. The next story illustrates how a person of the same age can have a much smaller net worth, yet be comfortable with having "enough" in a way that George was not.

Confidence Creates A Legacy

Steven was an 85-year-old widower who had two married children. He and his wife had sold their dry cleaning business several years before she died, had invested the proceeds wisely and lived modestly. After his wife's death, Steven focused his attention on his collections of coins and international travel with the Roads Scholar educational tours.

Steven's net worth was over $7,000,000 and he spent approximately $300,000 each year. His estate plan provided a generous inheritance to his two children as well as a significant charitable bequest to Steven's alma mater.

---

[1] *http://www.washingtonsblog.com/2013/05/have-more-people-lost-their-homes-than-during-the-great-depression.html*

He worked with his advisors to review his financial situation, and took great comfort in knowing that he was spending only income and not chipping away at principal. In fact, his estate was growing. He realized that if he ever decided to spend more, he could spend down some principal and still have plenty to pass on to his children. In fact, his advisors reassured Steven that he had plenty of money and could feel free to take more trips or make lifetime gifts to his children and alma mater.

The stories of Steven and George (and Mildred) illustrate how two eighty-five year olds can feel completely differently about their respective levels of financial security. The key to their feelings was confidence. Steven felt confident in his financial security while George and Mildred lived in fear of running out of money.

While we can attribute some of George and Mildred's fear to childhood experience, I believe that a good portion was due to a lack of trust in others, particularly an unwillingness to engage with professional advisors and solicit their input regarding financial and retirement planning. George and Mildred were victims of their own fears.

If you identify with George and Mildred, you are far from alone. Surveys indicate that running out of money is a common concern, even among the affluent. Rather than ignore or make light of that fear, I suggest that you do some introspection and confront it before engaging advisors.

Too often, spouses consult only each other. If one is a doomsdayer, that spouse can suck the other one down so they both become frightened of the future. They fuel each other's fears. Talking about the possibility of running out of money in a candid, objective manner with a close friend, sibling or adult child can halt this spiral and put fears into perspective. Often, with input from a trusted outsider, we can see the world more clearly. Once we identify and list realistic fears, we can bring that list to our professional advisors.

Concern about the future is completely normal, and it is important to acknowledge and express those concerns or fears to advisors—as both George and Steven did. Too often, we don't mention our fears to our advisors for reasons that range from embarrassment to a desire to avoid the extra fees that accompany spending time with an advisor. Believe it or not, advisors don't probe too deeply for similar reasons: they are reluctant to raise emotionally difficult topics and most are acutely sensitive to their clients' feelings about paying professional fees. Still, I argue that it is hugely important to your peace of mind, if you have fears, (and everyone does) that you bring them up to your advisors and give your advisors the opportunity to really listen, understand and help you work through them. Only through that process can you hope to gain confidence in your future financial security. When fears resurface (and they always do) your advisors can address your concerns on an ongoing basis and can tamp them down. And only by being aware of your fears can your advisors help you realistically confront them.

In summary, building a substantial net worth is not enough to be certain we will have "enough" for our financial security in our retirement years. Acknowledging and accepting that fear is a natural emotion and one we must confront and constantly address is essential. Going through an objective process and meeting regularly with outside professional help is the best way to build and retain confidence that you have "enough."

Step Five: Build Lasting Security and Lasting Confidence

I have come to believe that most of us will never feel fully financially secure if we try to achieve that confidence alone. Despite how irrational our fears may be, they are very real. Financial security is elusive—always requiring slightly more than we have! Advisors can bring rationality to our fears and reassure us. They help us turn problems into workable solutions. Without regular reinforcement from professional advisors we trust, our fears can take hold and take control of our decisions. Experienced advisors can shine a light on those fears as they arise, answer our "What If?" questions and even pose questions we haven't

…most of us will never feel fully financially secure if we try to achieve that confidence alone.

thought of. In doing so, they help us put fears in perspective and see the wisdom of the plans we've put in place for our financial security. In the coming pages we'll talk about how to build, and use, a team of advisors capable of answering your questions and providing the reinforcement you need.

Having confidence in the answer to "How much is enough for my financial security?" is absolutely necessary before we can move on the answer the next two questions:

1. How much is "enough," but not too much, for my children?

2. How do I leave a legacy to my children and community?

To see how one family regularly assures itself that it "has enough" read Chapter Seven "One Family's Legacy Plan."

Your advisors can help you gain and maintain your confidence. The reward to you is huge: you will live the last phase of your life not in a state of scarcity but of abundance.

WHERE ARE YOU ON THE FINANCIAL SECURITY SPECTRUM?

Place a checkmark beside the paragraph that most closely describes where you currently are on the financial security spectrum.

1. _____ We really don't know how much we spend or how much money we'll need in retirement. We should look into it.

2. _____ We think we know how much we'll need in retirement income. We have a goal to accumulate $_____ in savings by the time we retire.

3. _____ We have quite a bit of money. It should be enough, but who really knows? We worry about major medical bills, poor investment results and financial emergencies that could wipe out everything we've accumulated.

4. _____ The investment advisor who helps manage our money says we'll be fine in retirement. Our attorney updates our estate plan every five to six years. Our accountant prepares our tax return every year. When we need one of them for something, we call them.

5. _____ We have a professional advisor team that includes a retirement planning specialist, attorney and accountant. Working as a team, they have prepared a retirement plan and estate plan for us. We meet twice each year and make adjustments to our plans as necessary. They help us maintain our confidence that we can achieve all of our financial goals.

This is the first of several assessments to help you assess your answer to a particular question. In this case, the question is, "How much is enough?" Your answer above indicates where you are on a spectrum of possible actions related to confidence in your long-term financial security. This assessment and those that follow are part of creating your Legacy. I've provided a worksheet to calculate your development of your own Legacy Plan at the end of Chapter 8.

CHAPTER 3

How Much Is Enough, But Not Too Much, For My Children?

Success is to be measured not so much by the position that one has reached in life as by the obstacles which he has overcome.
BOOKER T. WASHINGTON

In the previous chapter, we learned how to determine how much is enough to sustain us during our retirement years and how to maintain confidence that we'll have enough over time. Now we can build on that foundation and have a meaningful discussion of the often-asked question, "How much should I leave my children?"

"Default" Estate Planning

You'll notice that his chapter title starts with the word, "How" instead of "Why" because traditional estate planning presupposes that we wish to leave our assets to our children. Every law firm's standard estate planning forms assume that your children will inherit your assets. Even if you die without a will, state intestacy laws distribute a portion of your assets to your children.

For those reasons, I refer to traditional estate planning as "default" estate planning. Default planning takes for granted that you wish to leave all (or nearly all) of your assets to your children. I'd ask you to take a step back and ask why? Specifically, why do we want to leave assets to our children?

Studies show that parents leave money to their children for a variety of reasons including to:

· **Express** feelings of affection

· **Preserve** family wealth

· **Carry** on a family tradition

· **Fulfill** a moral obligation

· **Minimize** taxes

In default estate planning, planners virtually never ask their clients, "Why do you want to leave assets to your children?" In fact, individuals planning their estates rarely ask themselves that question. It is simply the default assumption that if we have wealth, we want to pass it to our children. Understand that you have a choice. Examine, acknowledge and communicate the reasons for your choice to your advisors. This will help them customize a plan for you that achieves your specific goals.

When we were young and starting out, passing the little that we had to our children made perfect sense. Worrying that they would receive "too much" was the last thing on our minds!

Fast forward to today: We have accumulated more wealth than we thought possible when we first started out. Today, there will be enough left over upon our deaths to have a very dramatic effect on the children that will receive it. Yet, the basic template of our estate plans has changed little. While our plans are more complex, our default position remains the same: transfer all assets to our children.

As a result of the enormous wealth created in our country over the past 50 years, many wealth-holders are questioning this default position. When they ask themselves, "Why do I want to leave assets for my children?" they'll answer, "Because I love them." Many have come to believe, however, that too much money can be detrimental to their children's personal growth and happiness. The most prominent examples include: Warren Buffett, Bill Gates, Mark Zuckerberg and their spouses. Throughout this book you will find other wealth-holders who have come to similar conclusions.

The purpose of this chapter is to get you to challenge the default assumption. I want you to turn your focus inward and honestly answer the question, "Why do I want to leave money to my children?" To help you make that decision, I suggest that you use the Worksheet in the Appendix, *Why We Choose To Leave Money To Our Children*. Once you answer that question and, assuming you decide to leave your children something, it will be easier for you to grapple with the "how much?" question.

If you decide to leave a very large sum of money to your children, we will discuss how you might prepare them to handle it responsibly in Chapter 5. Alternatively, if you elect to leave them only enough to accomplish your goals for them, and leave the rest to a cause or organization in your community, we'll discuss those issues in Chapter 4. The key is that you pause and be thoughtful about the amount of money you wish to leave your children. Be deliberate and purposeful. Don't settle for default planning.

QUANTIFYING ENOUGH: A PROCESS TO DETERMINE HOW MUCH TO LEAVE CHILDREN

I have been asked, "How much money should I leave my children?" innumerable times. Typically, the question comes up in the context of an estate planning engagement, but not always. I've also been asked when playing golf, sitting at a college basketball game and a few times at cocktail parties. The question often comes from people I haven't worked with and whose children I don't even know! Do these folks assume that there is a "norm" that only professional advisors know about? Do they really expect me to say, "Oh, about $1,000,000" or "Two million dollars should be plenty!"?

Despite the naiveté of the question, it tells me that the person asking:
· **Cares** about their children.

· **Assumes** (since it is inherent in the question) that leaving too much money to children may actually be detrimental to their happiness and wellbeing.

They are right in assuming that leaving children "too much" money may do more harm than good. But soliciting the opinion of a professional advisor at a cocktail party is not the best way to determine the answer. The amount of money you decide to leave to your children is highly personal and depends on a number of factors related to your situation and to your children. It takes meaningful thought and dialogue between parents to arrive at an appropriate amount. Furthermore, this figure may change over time based on your net worth, competing interests for your money, your relationship with your children and their own financial situations.

I've created a process or exercise that you can use to answer the "How much do I leave to my kids?" question. I assure you that this process yields results that suit you and your family far better than those you'll receive via cocktail party opinions! Still this process is not prescriptive: there is no one right answer. For example, you know that each child is a product of his or her environment and life experience. An inheritance of $1,000,000 might be an incredible windfall for a child from one family, raised in one environment, but barely enough to cover a couple of years of expenses for another child raised in a very different environment. The process I propose here isn't going to yield a one-size-fits-all answer, but it will give you a framework for making the best decision for you and for your family.

This exercise has three primary benefits:

1. It stimulates meaningful dialogue between spouses and helps them "get on the same page."

2. It is a great tool to share with your estate planning advisors so they can tailor your plan to your goals.

3. It can be used to communicate with your children about your intentions and desires. You can do this in person or by letter, but communication can help set realistic expectations.

The Legacy Worksheet in the Appendix will help you with this exercise.

Step One: Ask All The Right Questions

Before you and your spouse set an inheritance amount that is appropriate for your family, I suggest you start with some introspection. You might begin with the following thought-provoking questions about your own situation, your children and your current plan about how to transfer your wealth.

Your Situation
  · What is your approximate net worth?
  · What is the nature of your assets (e.g. closely held business, farmland, commercial real estate, life insurance, securities)?
  · How old are you?
  · What is your estimated life expectancy?
  · How would you describe your relationship with your children?
  · What type of lifestyle do you live?

Your Children
  · How old are your children?
  · Are they all from the same marriage?
  · Are they single, married, divorced?
  · What career paths have they taken?
  · What type of lifestyle did your children grow up in?
  · What level of financial maturity have they exhibited to date?
  · How have they handled any significant cash gifts you have given?
  · Are they savers or spenders?
  · Do you meet with your children regularly?

Distribution Plans
  · Do you intend to leave an equal amount to each child?
  · Do you intend to transfer significant assets to your children during your lifetimes or only upon your deaths?
      ~ If at death, will you give to them outright or in trust?
      ~ If in trust, when will your children ultimately receive the assets?

Step Two: Clarify Your Intentions
   Most people are quite clear on what they do not want their children to spend their inheritances on. The most common items include:
   · Support a drug or illegal substance habit
   · Gambling
   · Prostitution
   · Extravagant lifestyle
   · Ability to avoid engaging in a meaningful career
   · Payments to a divorced spouse
   They are not as clear, however, about how they do want their children to spend their inheritances. The following list includes some

common acceptable items, but it is by no means exhaustive. Add your own items to it.

$_____	New(er) Home
$_____	New(er) Car(s)
$_____	Graduate School
$_____	Debt Reduction
$_____	Grandchildren's College Fund
$_____	Retirement Fund
$_____	Jewelry, Artwork, Collectibles
$_____	Foreign Travel
$_____	Early Retirement
$_____	Country Club Membership
$_____	Vacation Home
$_____	Investment Fund
$_____	"Do Whatever You Want" Fund
$_____	_____
$_____	_____
$_____	_____
$_____	Total

Step Three: Quantify Your Acceptable Item List

After you have identified the type of items you would like your children's inheritances to purchase, place a dollar amount or range next to each item. Total these numbers. It is important for spouses to be in agreement on both the items that appear on the list and the dollar amounts.

Step Four: Compare Before To After

Gaining a shared clarity with your spouse about exactly how much you wish to leave your children is a giant step in the planning process. The next step is to determine whether your current estate plan achieves those goals. To do so, ask your advisors to prepare a flow chart that illustrates who gets exactly what under your existing plan at each of your deaths. Compare the result with the goals you and your spouse have set.

Visualize how things will go under your current plan: if it were a movie, does it have a happy ending? Is your current plan reflective of the values you hold as parents? Many people are surprised by the discrepancy between the goals they identify using the Legacy Worksheet and the operation of their current estate plans.

If the amount parents calculate using the Legacy Worksheet is less than they expect, some people decide to increase the inheritance they will leave to their children. Many parents, however, discover that their existing estate planning documents provide their children with more than the total amount they calculated on the Legacy Worksheet.

Whether the total amount you calculate is more or less than you expected is not the point. The important thing is that you consciously make an informed decision

Studies confirm that most wealthy individuals…are concerned that leaving children too much money may be counter-productive.

about how much money to leave your children. Once you've made that informed decision you can develop a plan to prepare your children to receive the amount you desire and communicate with them about how you'd like them to use it.

Put It All Together

Studies confirm that most wealthy individuals want to pass some of their wealth to their children, but are concerned that leaving them too much money may be counter-productive. Knowing what the right amount is can be difficult to determine and is very personal.

If you want to leave money to your children, I hope that this exercise will help you clarify your motives for doing so. I am confident that the exercise will provide you insight into answering the "How much?" question for your family. Most importantly, the exercise puts you in charge and removes you from default planning mode. Finally, by thoughtfully answering the questions and inserting dollar amounts, you give your advisors the guidance they need to adjust your plan and documents to accomplish your goals.

ONE "ENOUGH" QUESTION AND FOUR DIFFERENT ANSWERS

The following stories illustrate how four sets of parents dealt with the how-much-to-leave-the-kids question. One relied on traditional (or default) planning to maximize a child's inheritance and minimize taxation without preparing the child to handle sudden wealth. Others took creative steps outside of the default-planning mode to prepare their children to receive inheritances of both money and family values.

The first story is about a father who did some great tax planning, but failed to instill his values in his son and communicate his wishes to him.

In the second story, two sisters with the same estate planning goals used very different strategies to meet their personal/family goals.

In the third story, a couple increased their giving to their three sons as their knowledge and maturity around wealth grew.

The last story involves a father who made it his second career to make his adult children financially literate and increased the amounts he left both to his children and charities.

The Case Of The Failed Inheritance

Max was a hard-charging guy who spent his entire career building a commercial storage business. Like many of us, he was no fan of taxes and dreamed that, one day, his only son Mitch and possibly Mitch's children, would inherit and run his business. So, upon the recommendation of his tax advisors, Max began to aggressively transfer shares of his company to Mitch. Max initiated this strategy when Mitch was in grade school, and continued it for more than 20 years.[2]

When Max died unexpectedly at age 62, Mitch's interest in the storage business was worth several hundred million dollars.

---

[2] *I believe it is important to distinguish between making Annual Exclusion gifts of cash ($14,000 per person in 2017) and gifts of non-voting stock in a family business. To pass a family business to successive generations it is often essential to gift stock consistently over many years to the next generation. Not making lifetime gifts of company stock can result in unnecessary taxation that can threaten the future viability of the business. There are two important differences between gifting shares in a business and making cash gifts. First, owning stock of a company typically brings no voting rights and the stock cannot be liquidated. Second, the parent/business owner normally works side-by-side with those children active in the business as a mentor with the opportunity to pass on values regarding wealth and money.*

Mitch, now age 30, stepped into the role of president and owner, and two years later stepped out of it—selling the company for cash.

Free from the "drudgery" of owning a business, Mitch devoted himself to spending his father's fortune. He began commuting between his multi-million-dollar homes on his private jet accompanied by various girlfriends and groupies. In essence, he retired in his 30s to a life that his father would not recognize, much less approve of. Today Max's son lives a life of the spoiled playboy. Nothing about what happened was part of Max's dream. In fact, it was truly Max's nightmare.

I find that "failed" inheritances are almost always attributable to a lack of communication. Too often, parents give money to children with no direction and then are disappointed in how children spend the funds. It's been my experience that most children will follow the wishes of their parents if those wishes are clearly communicated to them. A short story illustrates my point.

Same Goal. Very Different Outcomes

Two sisters, Jennifer and Elizabeth, ran an advertising agency. They had inherited the agency when their parents died in a tragic car accident years before. The two young women poured their hearts and souls into that business, building it into a regional dynamo over a 20-year period.

Having accumulated more net worth than they had ever imagined, Elizabeth and Jennifer sought the advice of a reputable estate planning attorney. This attorney pointed out that upon their deaths, each estate would have to pay significant estate taxes. To minimize that liability, he suggested:

- *Purchasing life insurance on their lives to both fund a buy-sell agreement and create a source of cash to pay the estate taxes.*

- *Begin the transfer of wealth to their children to reduce the value of the sisters' estates and shift wealth to the next generation. His reasoning was that since the children were the ultimate beneficiaries under the sisters' estate plans, why not transfer assets to them now and let the assets appreciate in the children's estates?*

The attorney advised Jennifer and Elizabeth that, under current law, each could make Annual Exclusion gifts of as much as $14,000 per year to each of their children. If their husbands also participated in the gifting, they too could give $14,000 to each child. Over years, the sisters and their spouses could transfer significant wealth to their children without paying any taxes.

Jennifer and Elizabeth had similar family situations: both were married and each had two children. In approaching their legacies, however, they tailored their own plans.

Elizabeth and her husband immediately began to give their children the maximum allowable amounts. At Christmas, each child received checks for $28,000 and an explanation that the gifts were part of their parents "tax planning."

After four years of "Christmas giving," Elizabeth and her husband returned to see their attorney for an estate plan check-up. When asked how the gifting program was going, Elizabeth shared that she was very unhappy with it. "The kids have blown it. They have used the money to buy fancy cars, take exotic vacations with friends and buy designer-label clothes." Elizabeth had lost some respect for her children and was frustrated with this aspect of tax planning!

The attorney was surprised to hear Elizabeth's story, not because he hadn't heard similar ones from other parents, but because he knew that Jennifer had had a completely different experience. "Why don't you talk to Jennifer about her gifting program?" he suggested.

Elizabeth did exactly that the following day. Jennifer told her how she and her husband had talked, before they started giving, about the goals they wanted to accomplish. In addition to shifting wealth and saving taxes, they wanted to teach their daughters (ages 17 and 19) about:

1. *Saving and investing.*
2. *Spending wisely.*
3. *Helping others who are less fortunate.*

Jennifer and her husband agreed to give $28,000 to each child each year, but decided to place those gifts into three buckets:

Bucket 1: An "investment" account that the children owned but that Jennifer controlled via voting rights. The purpose of the LLC was to hold investments that the family would make together.

Bucket 2: A "lifestyle" account to hold funds for the children to spend on items they wanted.

Bucket 3: A "charitable" account from which the children could disperse funds to the charities they chose.

Jennifer and her husband decided to allocate money into the three buckets as follows:

Year	Investment	Lifestyle	Charity	TOTAL
1	$18,000	$5,000	$5,000	$28,000
2	$16,000	$6,000	$6,000	$28,000
3	$14,000	$7,000	$7,000	$28,000

Jennifer explained to Elizabeth that she and her husband met with their children every six months for two to three hours to discuss the gifting. They reviewed the investments and performance. Each child reported on how she had spent funds in her lifestyle account and which non-profits she had decided to contribute to.

"The kids are learning about the basics of investing, saving and giving, but we're learning what items are most important to them through their lifestyle choices. We're also learning which causes they are passionate about," Jennifer told her sister. "We look forward to these meetings and are so proud of how both are learning to handle money responsibly."

Elizabeth (like Max) had done everything right from an estate-planning standpoint. Both had effectively transferred wealth and reduced their tax liability. Jennifer, however, had used tax planning as a platform for teaching her children valuable life lessons. In doing so, she gained the peace of mind that comes from knowing that when her children receive their inheritance, they will likely to have the skills, maturity, knowledge and experience to be prudent stewards of her estate.

Perhaps the best way to communicate your desires for your children is to put them in writing, then reinforce those wishes verbally, on a consistent basis. Families that have had the best experience are those who make a conscientious effort to pass on their values through regular family meetings focused on financial education.

This communication can take many forms. Think of the level of communication as a spectrum. You'll need to decide where you want to fall on the spectrum. The lowest level of communication is to leave a typical estate plan to be read only at your death. The children will assume that they are free to do whatever they decide with their share of inheritance.

The next level of communication is to write a personal letter to your heirs spelling out your desires and hopes. Children can then reference the letter in the future when pondering, "I wonder what Mom and Dad would have thought of this?"

A higher level of communication is to write a letter and talk to your children during your lifetime to clearly spell out your intentions.

The highest form of communication to one's children is best illustrated by two stories from our CAP® class speakers. In the first, we meet parents who incorporated philanthropy into the values they wanted to pass to their children.

Sowing And Reaping The Seeds Of Responsibility

Ralph and Susan had three sons. Ralph ran a very successful franchise business. Through stock options and prudent investing over many years, they accumulated a sizable estate.

When their sons were teenagers, Ralph and Susan decided to teach them financial literacy. Each year, on the day before

Thanksgiving, they would meet for two to three hours. Ralph always prepared an agenda. It was age-appropriate and changed each year. The early meetings focused on things like: saving for something they wanted (a bike, a stereo, a car, etc.); how compound interest worked (both for and against you); how to effectively use a credit card; how to save a portion of each paycheck. As they took jobs (part-time in college and full-time after college), the agenda included withholdings from paychecks (FICA, Medicare, federal and state income taxes, medical insurance, etc.), 401(k) plans, auto and homeowners insurance, mortgages, etc.

When all the boys were out of college, Ralph suggested the boys and Ralph prepare personal financial statements and compare them. At this time, Ralph and Susan began making significant cash gifts to their sons each year. The meetings then began to focus on how to invest, how to finance a home, how and when to incur debt and how to minimize income taxes.

Because the boys were accountable each year to compare their personal financial statements, they maintained family budgets and exercised financial discipline. The more responsible they became, the more money Ralph and Susan gifted them. They helped their sons save for their children's college education funds.

Today, the boys are in their forties. All are doing well. They still meet annually with their parents, Ralph and Susan. The agendas today focus on estate planning and charitable giving. Ralph and Susan have made it clear they feel they have given their sons enough. The balance of their estate will be left to various charitable causes.

A portion of Ralph and Susan's gifts each year is contributed to a donor advised fund at their local community foundation in each son's name. As a part of each annual meeting, each son reports on where his charitable dollars were distributed and why that charitable cause was important to him.

The annual pre-Thanksgiving Day meeting now is broken in two one-hour meetings. The first hour is just Ralph and Susan and their sons. They focus on personal financial statements and estate planning. The second hour includes spouses and grandchildren. The focus of that meeting is philanthropy.

While Ralph and Susan readily admit few families could compare personal financial statements each year without causing friction and resentment, it worked for them. The sons are all financially successful and truly like each other. Ralph and Susan take great satisfaction in the fact each son now holds a similar annual meeting with his children. After conducting these annual family financial meetings for over 25 years, Ralph and Susan are comfortable in the knowledge their sons will be good stewards of their wealth and are gratified by how the meetings have helped their family grow closer over the years.

Some people feel that, if they haven't taught their children how to handle money by the time the children finish school and move out of the house, it is too late. The following story involves a family whose adult children were out on their own—some living in cities far from their parents—yet who found a way to meet regularly to further their financial education.

Starting Late Is Better Than Not Starting At All

Phil had a background in finance and had served on the executive teams of two very large corporations. When the second company was sold, Phil found himself out of a job at age 60. He had plenty of money and energy, so he decided to "retire" to a second career. Part of that "career" would be to provide his four adult children the financial education necessary to prepare them to ultimately receive a sizable inheritance.

Phil gathered his four children (one son and three daughters between ages 30 and 40) and explained his plan. He would like them to meet with him and his wife every six months for one full day. The meetings would be on Saturday, start at 8:00 am *and finish after lunch. They would then spend the afternoon at their home and conclude with a dinner. Phil would pay the travel costs for children who lived out of town. Each child received a $500 board fee for attending.*

Phil had made many contacts over his years in finance. He called upon some of those contacts in his new "career." For each semi-annual meeting, he prepared a written agenda sent out in advance. Topics included a wide range of items dealing with finance. They included:

1. *Banking (how the FDIC works; securing the highest rate and lowest charges; how to borrow money effectively; establishing a line of credit, etc.);*

2. *Investing (definitions of financial instruments, mutual funds, asset allocation, taxation, money manager fees, risk-adjusted returns) and explaining how the stock market works;*

3. *Insurance (auto, homeowners, liability, life, disability, long-term care, commercial);*

4. *Taxation (income, payroll, federal, state, estate, inheritance, sales);*

5. *Accounting (personal financial statements, personal balance sheets, personal budgets, W-2s, K-1, 1099s);*

6. *Estate planning (wills, trusts, powers of attorney, living wills); and*

7. *Professional advisors (which ones you need; ways they are paid; how to use effectively).*

Phil covered some of the topics himself. However, he often invited former colleagues, advisors and vendors to address his children. When the guest speakers completed their presentations, Phil and his children would speak among themselves about what they learned. They would ask questions about how topics affected them personally.

Phil's wife, Mary Ann, sat in every meeting. She had never expressed an interest in financial matters since Phil had always handled their personal finances. However, Phil wanted Mary Ann to learn more about finance in the event he were to die before her or become incapacitated. With her four children in the room, Mary Ann was much more open to learning.

After lunch, Mary Ann always had a group activity planned. It could be touring a museum, hiking in a park, going to a movie, watching a football game on television, playing a board game, etc. The important thing was they spent those two days together every year.

Phil was able to use the knowledge he'd learned and the contacts he'd made over the years to provide financial education to his children. The children made a gift of their time to their parents and siblings. Together they grew stronger as a family.

After nearly 10 years of semi-annual meetings, Phil and Mary Ann felt comfortable sharing all of their personal financial information and estate plans with their children. They have placed their assets in trust and have their children serve as trustees. When Phil and Mary Ann pass away, there will be no surprises. The children know what there is, where it will go, how it will be managed, etc.

As the children learned more about finances and the parents gained more confidence in them, the amount Phil and Mary Ann determined to leave them increased.

As an interesting side note, after meeting for about five years, Phil and Mary Ann gifted $1,000,000 to an investment fund owned entirely and equally by the four children. The bylaws stated that the children could take distributions as needed, so long as all four children unanimously agreed. Phil was pleasantly surprised; no distributions were ever taken. Apparently, whatever pressing needs the children had were not so pressing after all! Today, the fund has more than doubled in size and continues to appreciate.

When presenting to our class, Phil brought two of his daughters. The class asked them about the value of the semi-annual meetings from their perspective. Neither had a financial background and admitted that some of the topics discussed were "above their heads." However, they said they are much more confident about money and finance and grateful for the education. Both have started mini-meetings with their small children to teach them the basics of personal budgeting and saving. Both agreed that what they cherished most about the semi-annual meetings was the quality time spent with their parents and siblings. They hope to continue the tradition even when their parents are no longer able to lead them.

A Commitment of Time

This chapter started with the question, "How much is enough, but not too much, for my children?" The lists that followed were designed to help you answer the question of why you would want to leave them any money at all. Once you considered all the reasons that you might want to provide an inheritance, you encountered several challenging questions to help you "back into" the dollar amounts that are appropriate for your family. Finally, you met four people who dealt with the question of legacy for themselves and their children.

The common theme to all of the stories, except Max's, is that all these parents wanted their money to do more. These parents did more than go to their attorneys' offices every few years to update their estate planning documents. They committed significant personal time and energy to talk to their spouses, examine their motives, meet with their children and communicate with them about financial matters.

If you want to be confident that you are leaving your children enough, but not too much money, and that they will use that money in accordance with your wishes, there is simply no substitute for clearly and regularly communicating your intentions through both your words and actions.

Finally, if you are tempted to dismiss the possibility of passing on your values because you think you or your children are too old to start now, or that you don't have enough financial knowledge to conduct family meetings, or that your children are too set in their ways, too distant, or simply uninterested, you may be right. Family meetings are not for every family. But you may be wrong. Family meetings can be very effective, and there are people who can help you organize them: your financial advisors, certain community foundations and nonprofit professionals. Before you decide whether family meetings will work for your family, I urge you to keep an open mind as you read the next chapter on philanthropy and the one following on conducting family meetings.

Where Are You On The Spectrum of Determining How Much Is Enough, But Not Too Much, For Your Children?

Place a checkmark beside the paragraph that most closely describes the actions you have taken to determine the amount of money (if any) you wish to leave to your children.

1. _____ I don't care what happens to my money after I die; I'll be dead. I haven't prepared an estate plan.

2. _____ I think my plan leaves everything to my spouse. I believe that if there is anything left, my kids will split it.

3. _____ We are concerned about the effects too big of an inheritance might have on our children so we've made certain that our money is held in trust until they are old enough to handle it. We haven't discussed our plans with our children.

4. _____ We think kids should make it on their own. We have talked about how much money to leave them and our plan gives them that flat amount at our death. The rest goes to charity. We haven't told our kids about our plan because we don't want them to be upset.

5. _____ We meet with our estate planning team annually. My spouse and I have consciously determined how much we will leave to our children, and how to distribute the balance to philanthropic causes that we care deeply about. We hold annual family meetings to provide guidance to our children and share our values with them. We have shared with our children how we'd like them to use the money and are confident that they will spend what we give them wisely. There will be no surprises when we die.

Your answer above indicates where you are on a spectrum of possible actions related to determining how much is enough to give your children. This assessment and those that follow are part of creating your overall Legacy Plan. To calculate your development toward your own Legacy Plan, move your answer to the worksheet at the end of Chapter 8.

CHAPTER 4

How Do I Leave A Legacy To My Children And My Community?

The measure of your life will not be what you accumulate, but in what you give away.
WAYNE DYER

Once you are confident that you have "enough" for your future financial security and you've decided how much money to leave your children, you can move on to the question of legacy. I like to think of legacy as connecting our money to meaning.

How will you be remembered after you are gone? Will people be inspired by your generosity to the community and those less fortunate? Will they admire the wonderful job you did raising caring, confident, contributing children? Or will you leave everything to children who will bitterly fight over or squander money they feel they were entitled to? Perhaps saddest of all, will you be forgotten because you really didn't make a difference?

My hope in writing this book is to help you leave a legacy to both your children and community. As you may have learned from the stories I've shared so far, the two—legacy to children and legacy to community—are often linked.

The stories in the previous chapter (Jennifer and Elizabeth, Ralph and Susan and Phil and MaryAnn) were about parents who left important legacies to their children. Not only did they leave them money, but they taught their children how to respect each other and work together. Parents taught children how to share their wealth with others less fortunate. These parents didn't simply hope that their children would be financially prudent, get along with each other and be generous. They modeled and consciously taught this behavior over time.

How will you be remembered after you are gone?

I have worked with parents who have become estranged from their children or unilaterally decided that they'd already given their children enough or that their children had made enough money on their own. When the parents died, their children were surprised and disappointed to learn that their parents had left all their assets to charities. The result was embittered children and disheartening (and expensive) litigation between siblings and the charities.

The balance of this chapter will focus on the legacy you might leave to your community. That legacy, however, should never be secured at the expense of your family legacy. In true legacy planning, the two—community legacy and family legacy—are melded. Ideally, you will work with your children in your philanthropic efforts. Even if you decide not to directly involve them in your efforts, you will model the behavior you would like them to emulate. Through ongoing communication and transparency, your children will absorb the lessons you teach.

Intentional Philanthropy

There are many people and organizations asking you for money to support their work. You've written many checks in response to those requests. While you are not unhappy that you responded, you did not find the process to be particularly fulfilling. Yes, the charities appreciated the cash, but you wonder if you really made a difference. I suspect that, like most of us, you would have given more if you were really passionate about the cause and the impact of your donation on real change.

If that's true, you are ready to transition from "checkbook philanthropy" to "intentional philanthropy." Intentional philanthropy occurs when you give money (and/or time) to a cause you find meaningful and that contribution is significant enough to make a positive difference.

No matter how you think about giving at this moment, meaningful giving is a journey, not a destination. Each of us takes a different journey complete with false starts, wrong turns and dead ends along the way. Each one of those "failures" brings a gift; the gift of experience.

Let's look how we typically think about leaving money to charity and then at all the options you truly have to connect your money to meaning.

Estate Planning And Giving To Charity

Early in my career as a fee-based financial planner, I asked people about their "charitable intent" just as I'd been taught. As a first step in the planning process, I used a formal written questionnaire (a "Fact Finder") to determine a person's needs and desires. The questions dealt with names, dates of birth, children's names, marital status, ownership of assets, etc. It's very likely that one of your advisors has asked you to complete this type of form at some point.

The "charitable intent" question I asked was, "Do you intend to include charity in your estate plan?" Not wanting to appear judgmental, I would ask the question using the same voice as I would, "What is your current address?" Clients would typically answer the "charitable intent" question in one of four ways:

1. "No."
2. "I don't think so."
3. "We haven't talked about it."
4. "We'll let you know."

The fact of the matter is, few of us think about leaving a charitable legacy until someone asks us, and the first time that question comes up is usually in a meeting with our estate planning attorney.

Re-phrasing The Charity Question

Today, I ask the charitable question differently, and I rarely hear one of those four responses. Have my clients' attitudes toward charitable giving changed? I don't think so. Rather, I believe I help them articulate what they want to do, but just haven't put into words, much less action.

What do I do differently? First, my preparation for client meetings has changed. I typically ask to see a couple's recent income tax return either in advance or at our first meeting. Today, I look at the Charitable Deduction line a little differently. If I find (as I usually do) that a couple has been quite generous, I ask them about the nonprofits and their connection to them. If they express a strong affinity to one or more, I tuck this information away for later in the discussion.

Second, I no longer limit myself to the questions on a generic "Fact Finder." I ask where each person grew up, went to high school and college. I ask about their children and where they attended high school and/or college and if they had a good experience. I ask whether they do volunteer work and if so, where.

When we discuss the distribution of assets later in the meeting, I may say something like, "From your income tax return, it's obvious that you've been quite generous with XYZ charity. No doubt they will miss your generosity when you're no longer alive. If it works within your plan, and we can do so tax efficiently, would you be interested in learning about how your gifts might continue after you're gone?" Or, "It sounds like you and your spouse have fond memories of your alma mater. Has anyone ever shown you how you can leave whatever is left in your IRA upon your death to your alma mater (or any charity of your choosing), and have the federal government essentially match your gift?"

When approached in this manner, most people are intrigued and want to know more. More often than not, they decide to include one or more charitable organizations in their estate plans.

Once a person decides to include charity in their estate plan, they assume that they only need to name a charity and an amount. While these are important decisions, your work is not done.

· Are you passionate about a specific cause (literacy, the environment, animals, healthcare, etc.)?

· Are you comfortable having your donation added to the organization's general fund?

· Do you want to restrict your gift to specific purposes?

· Would you like to set up your own "foundation" now or upon your death and have the foundation make distributions each year?

· Should the foundation be perpetual or should it "sunset" at some time in the future?

· Would you prefer to make your gift in a single lump sum or spread gifts over a number of years?

· What about your children? Have you thought about including them in your philanthropy? Depending on their age and interest, letting them have a say in which organizations receive some of your charitable dollars could teach them compassion and good citizenship.

This is a great opportunity to accomplish something important – to leave a charitable legacy that is meaningful to you. There are resources available such as development officers or community foundations that would be happy to help you sort through all your options at no charge to you.

Becoming An Intentional Philanthropist

Using your estate plan to give to charity rather than waiting for the right cause to pull at your heartstrings, puts you in the driver's seat. After all, it is your life to which you are trying to give meaning! If you aren't sure how to connect your money with meaning, do some introspection.

· Who has formed you?

· What organizations (schools, church, scouting, Boys or Girls Club, etc.) have impacted you?

· What injustices would like to address?

· What behaviors (leadership, mentoring, volunteering, etc.) would you like to reinforce and see fostered?

· Do you have close friends or family members who have strong connections to causes or organizations that are important to you as well?

Take some time assembling your list of the organizations or causes you want to benefit from your generosity. Revisit it periodically. Understand that your list may change over time. That's perfectly normal.

Reach out to these organizations to learn more about them. This might include doing some online research, requesting literature from them, asking others what their experiences with them have been or personally visiting the organization. Other good sources that are familiar with most of the non-profits in their communities are the United Way (social services) or your community foundation.

You will quickly learn that there are far more worthy organizations that could use your support than you have resources. Don't let that imbalance overwhelm you. You can't possibly solve everyone's problems, but you can prioritize your list of worthy organizations based on your interests and passions.

Almost always, you will find giving to be far more rewarding when you choose a few causes or organizations and contribute a meaningful number of dollars to them rather than sprinkle small numbers of dollars to a large number of organizations.

...you will find giving to be far more rewarding when you choose a few causes or organizations and contribute a meaningful number of dollars...

THE GIFT OF TIME

So far, I've talked only about gifts of money, specifically, how to give your dollars (during lifetime or at death) to a limited number of organizations in order to amplify your contributions. But you have more than financial resources to give. *The gift of your time and/or leadership may be worth more than money.* The more engaged you become the more rewarding it will be for you. By committing your energy and efforts to a few organizations you feel passionate about, the easier it will be to turn down other requests for money without guilt. In other words, the stronger your, "Yes," the easier it is to say, "No."

Too often I've witnessed people who've been incredibly generous with their time and money feel inadequate because they couldn't say "yes" to everyone who asked them for money. Being purposeful about your philanthropy can be empowering and leave you with the knowledge you've done your best. Whether you have millions or billions, it is not enough to meet all of the needs. By developing a focused plan that combines your passion and leadership, and is implemented with compassion, you will achieve a new level of contentment and self-satisfaction.

Some intentional philanthropists incorporate philanthropy in their estate planning not only as a way to give of their time and money, but also as a conduit to pass on their values and build stronger families. Letting children know which causes and organizations you contribute to provides them insight into what is important to you. Letting your children designate a portion of your charitable dollars provides you insight into what causes are important to them. Combining the two can be a teaching platform and a powerful way to strengthen the ties that bind you.

Let me share a story of what one wise matriarch did to pass her values on to her grandchildren.

A Matriarch Passes The Torch

"Madge" was about 80 years old and blessed with many grandchildren. They were dispersed throughout the region and she did not see them as often as she would have liked. She and her late husband ("William") had always been very generous and she wanted to pass "the gift of giving" to her grandchildren.

With the help of a charitable advisor, Madge announced she was establishing a "board of directors" among her grandchildren. To be on the board, a child must be at least eight years old. Once a child turned 21, they "aged out" and must resign from the board.

Madge held two board meetings per year: one was at her home and the other at her vacation home. The meetings lasted about two hours.

The family's wealth came from a third-generation banking business. Each meeting started with a brief presentation by Madge's son, the bank's president. He would, in "age-appropriate" terms, discuss the prior year and whether or not the bank made a "profit." For if the bank did not make a profit, there would be no money to share with those in need. Based on profitability, it was determined how much could be given away that year.

Upon joining the board each child was given a packet about the etiquette expected in board meetings. In fact, every child was expected to read Robert's Rules of Order. A president, vice president and secretary were elected for one-year terms. Each child eventually rotated through the offices.

Madge would typically choose five to six separate causes she wanted to give to that year. However, the board could choose only three. They must also decide how much to allocate to each. The causes might include: the zoo, the fire department, the Humane Society, Boy or Girl Scouts, etc. With the help of the charitable consultant, the children went on field trips and/ or had the nonprofits come to their meetings.

These meetings have been going on for over six years. The children have learned there are people and organizations that are not as economically blessed as they are. They learned it is difficult to decide which organization to give to when all seem worthy. They discovered that when acting in a group they must be persuasive to make their point. They also learned to compromise, cooperate and disagree agreeably.

The children learned "profit" is a good thing and provides more to share with others. They were learning the basics of business and good citizenship all while growing closer to their siblings and cousins.

The idea for this "board of directors" came from an advisor who was helping Madge and William complete their estate plan. Once they determined to leave "something" in their wills for charity, Madge asked, "Why do we have to wait until we die?" She came up with the idea of connecting with her grandchildren now. With the help of a charitable consultant, together they developed the business model for their family philanthropy.

Today two children have "aged out." The youngest is now eight, so all children are or have been on the board. The consultant prepares the agenda, helps facilitate the meetings, keeps the minutes and follows through on action steps. Madge gets to spend time with her grandchildren and takes great pride in watching them grow into a caring, cohesive family.

Obviously, this is a significant commitment of time, energy and money on Madge's part to make this work. I am not suggesting this would work for everyone. By using one's imagination, however, a plan might be developed that fits your own family. Certain community foundations and charitable consultants may be available to help you in your own community.

When determining if you want to include charity in your planning, an important question is, "Why would I give?" Your answer will be unique to you. However, a common theme emerged from the many speakers who addressed our CAP® Study Groups: Gratitude.

While expressed slightly differently by each presenter, each felt incredibly blessed. They realized that while their success was a result of hard work, many other factors were involved: the values their parents instilled in them; the country they were born in; the teachers who educated them; the bosses who nurtured and mentored them; the challenges that made them stronger; the support of their spouses; etc. In short, each felt a strong sense of gratitude and an obligation to give back.

Your motivation may be gratitude. It might be to save taxes or create a forum for your children to work together, fulfill a commitment you made to your community; or a combination of these or other reasons. Acknowledging your own motivation can help determine what form your giving might take.

In the preceding chapters we discussed gaining the confidence necessary to live the final third of our lives in abundance rather than scarcity. I suggested that we do that through knowing we have enough money for our financial security, both today and in the future. We also talked about being purposeful in deciding how much of an inheritance to leave our children.

In this chapter we talked about leaving a legacy both to our children and community. In giving to our communities, I outlined the process of becoming an "intentional" philanthropist by narrowing our charitable giving to those causes that are most compelling to us. Giving our time and leadership can be equally gratifying to the giver and receiver. Including our children and grandchildren in our philanthropic efforts can provide a positive forum to transfer our values to children and deepen our relationships.

On the following page, determine where you currently fall on the Legacy Spectrum. If that point is not where you want to be, it is my hope that you will use some of the ideas in this chapter to take you to that point.

Where Are You On The Spectrum Of Creating A Legacy For Your Community?

Place a checkmark next to the paragraph that most closely describes the community legacy you have created.

1. _____ We don't give money to charity and have not included any non-profit organizations in our estate plans. Charity begins at home.

2. _____ My spouse and I make small gifts to various charitable organizations on occasions when we are asked. We haven't given any thought to including charities in our estate plan.

3. _____ We feel that we are more generous than most, and plan to leave something to charity the next time we update our wills.

4. _____ The last time we updated our estate plan we made provision for several charities we care about. We didn't tell the charities involved and have not thought about telling our children about what we have done or why.

5. _____ With the help of a charitable consultant, we have written a philanthropic plan. That plan sets out our goals and establishes parameters for the dollars we will commit to charity both during and after our lifetimes. At our annual family meetings, we include our children in our philanthropy, allowing them to designate some funds to causes they care about. Ultimately, our children will help carry out our philanthropic plan when we die. During our lifetimes, we are committed to devoting our time, talents and treasure to causes we feel strongly about.

Your answer above indicates where you are on a spectrum of possible actions related to creating the legacy you wish to leave to your community. This assessment is part of creating your overall Legacy Plan. To calculate your progress toward developing your own Legacy Plan, move your answer to the worksheet at the end of Chapter 8.

Whether to "do your own thing" or include your children in your philanthropy is a decision only you can make. Donors who involve their families often feel that they are leveraging their philanthropic dollars by growing a new generation of philanthropists: their children.

Family philanthropy is often a part of family meetings: the topic of the next chapter.

CHAPTER 5

Blueprints For Passing Down Values

Educating the mind without educating
the heart is no education at all.

ARISTOTLE

I f you've reached this point, I assume that you have some interest in or curiosity about the idea of preparing your children to inherit money. I hope I've made my case that preparation may involve:

- **Educating** children to handle money responsibly.

- **Communicating** to them the principles and values you'd like to see them employ as they work together managing and consuming the money.

- **Sharing** with them your interest in and involvement with charitable causes.

I've found, through both my own family experiences and the stories of others, that the best way to accomplish any, or all, of those goals is to hold family meetings.

HOLDING EFFECTIVE FAMILY MEETINGS

Many parents like the idea of family meetings. They visualize their children looking forward to getting together, learning from them and sharing with siblings. They imagine their children smiling and can almost hear the laughter as family stories are shared.

Unfortunately, these blissful thoughts can dissolve as doubts begin to set in. What if my children don't want to come? Will they think family meetings are a stupid idea? What if they don't get along during the meeting? Where would we have the meeting? How long should it last? Who will lead it? What should the agenda be? Should we invite their spouses?

It is normal to experience doubts about any new venture we initiate. The most difficult step, however, is the first one. If you decide to hold family meetings, do some initial preparation, then just do it.

If you decide to hold family meetings, do some initial preparation, then just do it.

Every family has its own unique dynamic. You may have one child or ten. They may live next door to you or be dispersed throughout the world. Some may get along with their siblings better than others. Children may be married, single, divorced, or have life partners. It doesn't matter. All that matters is that they are your children.

Family meetings that include teenagers will obviously be different from those involving a 50-year-old child. If you are widowed, your family meeting will not be the same as one hosted by a couple. That too doesn't matter. You simply need to start from where you are today.

Meeting Preparation

Step 1: Set Your Goals

Perhaps the most important first step to holding successful family meetings is to be clear on what your goals are for holding the meeting in the first place. Your goals are unique to your family and you may have one goal or many. Whatever goals you set, put them in writing and prioritize them. Only once you are clear on what you hope to accomplish do you communicate your goals to your children. The key is to be clear with yourself and your children about what you are trying to accomplish.

Here is how one family I work with prioritized its goals:

- **Build** a forum where we might develop stronger loving relationships with each other so we can work well together when we must make difficult family decisions.

· **Pass** on to our children our personal values through stories and experiences.

· **Share** with our children some of our personal financial and estate planning decisions.

· **Provide** the financial education our children need to be good stewards of the inheritance they will receive.

Step 2: Create The Meeting Format

· **Prepare** an agenda. Once you determine your goals, you can create the agenda for the meeting,

· **Choose** a facilitator for your meetings. That might be you, one of your children or an outsider. Your local community foundation may offer meeting-facilitation support. Alternatively, you can hire one of your professional advisors. (Will this person take minutes and follow up on any action items? If not, determine who will.)

· **Set** ground rules. For example: Will you allot time to each child to speak? Can speakers be interrupted? If so, for what purposes? How long will meetings last?

· **Consider** expenses. If travel is involved, will children pay their own travel expenses to attend meetings or will you reimburse them? Some families pay a "Board of Directors" stipend to offset travel expenses and encourage attendance. (A little financial incentive may kick-start your children's enthusiasm for meetings and keep them coming!)

· **Decide** whether (or not) to include in-laws. Most families choose to include only children during their initial family meetings. After several meetings (or however many it takes to establish a rhythm) they add in-laws. This choice depends on your family's dynamics, relationships and the individuals involved. My best counsel on this topic is: Go slowly.

· **Create** a file for each child to store meeting agendas, minutes, notes and any required follow-up information.

· **"Go live"** if philanthropy is one of your agenda items. That is, you might invite each child to donate a sum of money (that you provide) to a charity of their choosing. At your family meeting, you will ask children to share with the group why they chose to give to the organizations they did. In this exercise parents and children learn much about each other's values and passions.

Step 3: Communicate With Your Children

When you propose the idea of family meetings to your children, you will share with them your goals for holding meetings in the first place. Then:

· **Ask** each child for his or her preferences on dates and times for family meetings. Everyone has limited time. You are competing with their careers, spouses, and your grandchildren's soccer schedules and school events.

· **Accommodate** your children's needs. If one of your children lives abroad or too far away to make travel practical, remember technology is a wonderful thing. Better to hold a meeting via Skype or FaceTime than hold no meeting at all.

· **Invite** each child individually to the family meeting and ask for their help in making meetings successful.

· **Send** a written agenda to children in advance of each meeting.

· **Thank** each child after meetings, in writing, for attending, and remind them of any follow-up actions and the date of the next meeting.

Step 4: Improve Your Odds For Success

Through experience, I've found that parents can assume attitudes that will improve the odds that the family meetings they hold will achieve their goals. These include:

· **Be flexible.** If you don't complete the entire agenda, but meet some (or all) of your goals, you've succeeded!

· **Be patient.** Just because you hold a well-planned, "formal" meeting, participants suddenly do not behave differently or check their personalities at the door. Your son who speaks before he thinks or daughter who is sensitive to any perceived slight will behave no differently in a family meeting. All of us, especially children, are works in process. Children are maturing and that takes time.

· **Expect disputes**. It is perfectly normal for siblings to disagree and for children to disagree with parents. Harsh words can be part of the process of reaching decisions and part of family life, but they need not set the tone. Model the behavior you expect from your children and use a reminder of your goals to bring everyone back on track.

· **Share responsibility.** Success depends on both you and your children so allow them—no—direct them to assume leadership roles as appropriate.

Step 5: Meeting Tips

Once the meeting begins engage everyone. Ask open-ended questions like:

· What is going on in your life right now or what was the most exciting thing that happened in your life since our last meeting?

· What is/was your biggest disappointment?

· What do you feel is the best attribute that you bring to our family?

· What is one thing you feel you could do to be a better sibling/person?

Have fun. It's all about the journey!

My Family's Meetings

My first experience with family meetings was a personal one. It began years ago with a family corporation. First, some background. My mother and father were both raised in the Midwest, each in large Catholic families of very modest means. Neither attended college. During grade school, my father was hired out to a neighboring farm and never had the opportunity to attend high school. Nevertheless, through years of hard work he built a successful automobile dealership.

A number of years ago (when the Lifetime Exemption was $600,000 and the top estate tax rate 55%), my dad's tax advisor encouraged him to begin gifting assets to his eight children to avoid paying estate taxes. While my father had no intention of giving up lifetime control of his money, he abhorred the idea of paying federal estate taxes. Reluctantly, he set up a family corporation. He and my mother held the only voting shares. Each year, through Annual Exclusion Gifts (of up to $10,000 per child), they transferred non-voting shares to their children.

My father asked me to run the corporation's annual shareholder meetings. In the early years, meetings lasted only about an hour during which my father did almost all of the talking. He reported on how the business and investments had performed that year. There wasn't much discussion.

Then a funny thing happened. As we became familiar with both the format and our parents' expectations, we began to relax. We started asking questions about our parents' estate plan. The meetings began to stretch out to two, and sometimes three, hours. After the initial "business" portion of the meetings my mother and father would often tell us stories about their younger years—stories we'd never heard before. Soon everyone would share childhood memories. In my family there is a 22-year gap between the youngest and oldest siblings. Meetings provided an opportunity for us younger kids to get to know our older siblings. Inevitably, there was much laughter, and occasionally a few tears, as we shared each other's triumphs and pain.

Our family meetings continued for over 20 years. My parents scheduled the meetings just before the annual Weber Family Reunion held each summer for over 40 years. The strong bonds of trust we built in those annual meetings served our family well. Friends and acquaintances marveled at how well we got along when our parents died and as we settled their estate.

While our family meetings started out as a formal corporate procedure, they turned into much more. They provided us financial education. We learned about borrowing money, interest rates, taxation, depreciation, investments, insurance, lease agreements, employee benefits, dealing with bankers and much more. While my parents had always lived lives of frugality, modesty and hard work, family meetings provided them the opportunity to talk about why those values were important to them. Our family meetings were the one opportunity we had to talk as adults without the distraction of grandchildren or spouses. We grew in our friendship as siblings. Our family meetings became a sort of "glue" that brought and held our family closer together.

Not too long ago an acquaintance told me that she had tried a family meeting, but "it didn't work." I asked her to tell me more.

Meeting Failure or Lesson Learned?

"Louise" asked her attorney to help her with her first family meeting so he sent a letter inviting her four children to meet in his office at the time he and Louise had chosen.

At the outset of the meeting Louise announced her attorney would tell the children about her estate plan.

The attorney spent about an hour explaining the technicalities of Louise's estate planning documents. When he finished, he asked if the children had any questions. The youngest timidly raised her hand and asked a question. Her older brother jumped in and answered the question in a way that made her feel silly for asking. His response had the predictably chilling effect and inhibited any further questions. With no questions to ask and nothing else to add, Louise called the meeting to an end. She left disappointed about the lack of interaction and dismayed that her children didn't get along better. She wasn't sure she would try another family meeting.

How might this situation have turned out differently?

Clarify Goals. The only goal Louise shared with her attorney was to share her estate plan, yet she was disappointed when her family meeting accomplished that goal. Obviously she had other goals but she didn't communicate those to her attorney or to her children. Be clear on your reasons to hold family meetings (e.g., financial education, passing on values, family camaraderie, etc.).

Seek Input. Louise set the meeting time and date based on her schedule and that of her attorney instead of asking her children which dates and times might work best for them. She unwittingly chose the same date as her son's annual golf game with his high school friends. Not surprisingly, her children (and especially her son) viewed her "invitation" as a mandate. If Louise holds future meetings, she might seek her children's input on both dates and agenda.

Personalize The Invitation. Louise let the attorney issue the invitation instead of personally inviting each child face-to-face or by phone. She failed to share with them her intent and hopes for the meeting. She never asked for their help in making it successful.

Meet In A Comfortable Setting. She didn't realize that holding a meeting in an attorney's office can be off-putting or stifle the informal flow of conversation. I would have suggested that she hold the meeting in her own home or in a vacation home.

Use An Informal Format. Louise's attorney viewed this meeting as he would any other client meeting and dressed the part. If you invite your professional advisor to a family meeting, ask them to dress casually and let them know that you want them to be informal and facilitate discussion.

As Louise discovered, the first family meeting may not meet all of your expectations, much less be a resounding success. Don't be discouraged. Family meetings are new to you and your children. Admittedly, formal meetings about topics you may never have discussed with your children can be somewhat uncomfortable, but if you openly share the reasons for holding them and what you hope to accomplish, your first meeting could be the start of a process and discussion that will last many years.

What's In It For The Kids?

We've talked about all the great reasons parents have to hold meetings, but what motivates our children to participate? When we first initiate family meetings, I think it is always helpful not just to communicate our goals but also to appeal to our children's self-interest. We are asking them to give us their time, so we can expect them to ask themselves, "What's in it for me?" A meeting agenda can answer that question. As appropriate to your goals and family, you might include:

Annual Gifting. If you decide to make gifts of cash or assets to your children, the family meeting would be an ideal place to do it.

Education Funding for Grandchildren. If you choose to fund all or part of your grandchildren's college expenses (i.e., 529 Plans, trusts, etc.), the family meeting is a good time to talk about: funding, investment results, tax consequences, grandchildren's college intentions, etc.

Philanthropy. Many families incorporate philanthropy as a standing meeting agenda item. Discussing charitable activities can be enlightening, heartwarming and a great way to learn about each other's passions.

As you think about holding family meetings, remember that logistics are merely details to be worked out. The most important decision is the decision to regularly communicate with your children. Meetings have a structured format. They provide a forum to share ideas, opinions and values. Through meetings you create an environment for discussion that is warm and inviting. The gift of your time and the sharing of your "stories" may ultimately be a more important gift than the money you plan to leave them.

Conclusion

I've listed a number of topics that you might include in your family meetings at the end of this chapter. I'm sure you'll add to the list. To make meetings most effective, however, it is critical to: 1) clearly define what you hope to accomplish and 2) tailor them to the financial sophistication of your children.

If you are a 70-year-old widow and your children are 45 and 40 and are both financially savvy, your meetings might focus on specific assets and estate planning issues. Alternatively, if your meetings include grandchildren and your intent is to educate them on how to accumulate and preserve wealth, your delivery and level of detail would be dramatically different.

If family meetings are new to you, expect some missteps and don't be afraid to experiment. Your children may be afraid to talk initially for fear of appearing stupid in front of siblings and advisors. It will take time and patience to build the necessary trust for open, honest learning to take place. Keep it informal and make everyone comfortable. Invite guest speakers when they can bring specialized knowledge and enhance the family's learning, but make certain that they talk at a level that is appropriate to your children.

There will be no tests to evaluate which family members "mastered" the information. Some meetings will be more productive than others. You will get sidetracked at times when the family wants to share a story or experience unrelated to your topic. Occasionally, there may be disagreements between children in which you are awkwardly caught in the middle. These are a natural part of all family dynamics.

If one of your goals was to promote family unity, awkward moments are great "growth" opportunities. You are a parent, not a psychologist. It is not critical to complete your entire agenda. Learning to disagree agreeably or coaxing a festering problem out into the open is more important than children learning the intricacies of insurance or investing. Ideally, your family has committed to regular meetings so, if necessary, you can pick up where you left off at the next meeting. Building strong family bonds today may avoid heartbreak and litigation when your estate is settled.

When managed properly, family meetings can be very rewarding to you as you see your family members work together for common goals.

Where Are You On The Spectrum Of Passing Your Values To Your Children?

Place a checkmark next to the paragraph that most closely describes how you communicate with your children about money, estate planning and your family's values.

1. _____ We really don't get together as a family. We all live our separate lives.

2. _____ We occasionally get together for funerals or weddings, but our gatherings are superficial because everyone does not get along.

3. _____ Our family does get together several times per year but we consider each family's finances to be very personal and do not talk about them.

4. _____ We get along well with all of our children and their spouses and have shared with them, in general terms, how our estate will be distributed.

5. _____ We hold meetings with our children annually with the express purpose of: 1) discussing our estate plan; 2) clarifying our personal values; and 3) spelling out our expectations of them.

Your answer above indicates where you are on a spectrum of possible actions related to passing your values on to your children. This assessment is part of creating your overall Legacy Plan. To calculate your progress in developing your own Legacy Plan, move your answer to the worksheet at the end of Chapter 8.

SUGGESTED TOPICS FOR FAMILY MEETINGS

Communication is essential in an effective handoff of wealth and values between generations. Holding family meetings provides an excellent forum for this communication. They are held face-to-face with all stakeholders in one room. They can be emotionally charged and bring out the best, and occasionally the worst, in family dynamics.

Having clearly communicated goals and a long-range perspective will be instrumental in making your family's meetings productive and rewarding to all participants.

After you have: 1) set your goals (concise, written and shared with your children); 2) created the meeting format (location, facilitator, agenda, participants, time and date); and 3) effectively communicated with your children (personal invitation to a meeting that accommodates their schedules, whose purpose they understand and in which their input is key to success), it is important to address relevant topics.

Everyone can be expected to be a bit wary for the first few meetings so consider starting with some "ice-breaker questions" to warm up your audience. You might ask participants to take ten minutes to jot down answers to:

1. In the past year, what is the best thing that happened to:
   · Your family?
   · Your career?
   · Your health?

2. In the past year, what is the worst thing that happened to:
   · Your family?
   · Your career?
   · Your health?

3. In the next 12 months, what are you most looking forward to:
   · Your family?
   · Your career?
   · Your health?

At the end of ten minutes, ask each to read their answers aloud. In doing so, everyone has a quick snapshot of what is happening in everyone else's life.

Warm-up Tips:

- **Provide** everyone paper, pen and the written questions at the beginning of the meeting.

- **Ask** participants to hold questions or comments for each speaker until a designated time during or after the meeting.

- **Feel** free to modify the questions for your family or give participants more (or less) time to write their answers.

The point is to create a "warm-up" period that allows everyone to relax a little and become somewhat vulnerable by sharing something about themselves. Effective warm-ups lay the groundwork for meaningful dialogue.

Meeting Style

No one likes to be lectured to or patronized. After the first couple of meetings, you may want to begin introducing certain financial topics to enhance the financial literacy of your children. Obviously, the timing and content is highly dependent on the age and financial acumen of your children. Your children may have vastly different levels of knowledge and interest in certain topics.

Meetings are not classes. There are no tests to assess each person's grasp of the information presented. Rather, meetings provide an opportunity for you (and your children) to share personal data and examples. This is your chance to pass on your values and life lessons. For example, instead of simply declaring, "Everyone should have 90 days of after-tax spendable income in an emergency fund" consider sharing an example from your early career in which an emergency fund saved you from having to sell your home, apply for food stamps or declare bankruptcy. By using your personal stories, the points you are making come to life and make a greater impact on your children.

You might ask your children to provide input on certain topics in which they have specialized knowledge. Use your professional advisors as well—after you have coached them about your goals and their presentations. (Beware: Advisors can easily become too detailed and technical when given the chance to present topics to your children.)

Certain community foundations and non-profit organizations may be able to provide trained meeting facilitators if you are not comfortable doing so yourself.

Below I have listed some topics you might include in your family meetings. Assuming your meetings last two to three hours, you may only cover one or two topics per meeting. Think in terms of five to ten annual meetings when planning your agenda. Taking this longer view may prevent you from cramming too much information into too few meetings and overwhelming your children.

There may be times when your meetings are sidetracked and don't cover all agenda items. If one of your meeting goals is to encourage family unity and, although "sidetracked" your children are sharing with each other, you've accomplished your goal! You can defer the technical agenda items to the next meeting. Learning to work together as adults can be far more important in the long run than becoming technical experts in any one topic!

These topics are but a few of the many you can include in family meetings. Be patient. It takes time to cover the territory and time to develop trust among family members. The most important part may be your persistence and willingness to appreciate each child's differences and contributions. Your family is unique. Your children are unique. Appreciate all of it as you begin your journey to becoming a closer, grounded, well-adjusted family. Practice in this area may not make perfect, but it does make better!

Trusts

1. What are they?

2. How and why are they used?

3. What is a trustee?
   A. What are trustee responsibilities?
   B. How is a trustee paid?
   C. Who should be asked to be a trustee (corporate vs. individual)?

4. How we have used trust(s) in our estate plan
   A. Are they funded or unfunded?
   B. Who will be the trustee?

C. What are the provisions?

D. When and how can money be distributed from them?

E. How will the trust be taxed?

Recommendation: Consider inviting a bank trust officer to address your family to explain how they: 1) typically invest money, 2) gather, account for and manage all assets after a death, 3) determine who gets distributions, and 4) have had to decline requests for distributions.

Taxation

1. Ordinary income tax

2. Capital gain tax

3. Transfer taxes
   A. Gift
   B. Estate

4. Step-up in basis

5. Entities including "pass-thru"

6. Taxation of:
   A. Trusts and trust distributions
   B. Qualified retirement plans
   C. Inherited assets

7. Charitable deductions
   A. Lifetime
   B. Bequests

8. Taxes at our deaths
   A. Who pays (apportionment)?
   B. Who figures out all this?
   C. Steps we have taken in our estate plan to minimize taxes

Recommendation: Consider inviting your accountant or tax attorney to address these topics.

Social Security and Medicare

1. What are these programs?
   A. When did they start?

    B. How are they funded?

    ~ Give examples of payroll taxes.

    C. What are the benefits?

  2. How does one qualify for benefits?

    A. When should one apply for benefits?

    B. How much will the benefits be?

  3. What is a Medicare Supplement policy?

  4. How does this affect us?

Recommendation: Consider inviting your financial planner to address these topics.

Insurance

  1. Automobile and Homeowners

    A. Our levels of coverage

    B. Our reasons for coverage

    C. Children's levels of coverage

  2. Personal Liability Insurance

    A. What does it cover?

    B. How much should someone typically have?

    C. Approximately how much does "typical" coverage cost?

  3. Life

    A. What is life insurance?

    B. Why do people have it?

    C. How much should one have?

    D. What types of polices are there?

    E. At death:

      1. How is money (proceeds) paid out?

      2. Who do proceeds go to?

      3. How are proceeds taxed?

    F. Can anyone qualify for life insurance?

    G. How much does it cost?

    H. What is the best way to buy it?

    I. Our life insurance

      1. How much we have

      2. Our reasons for purchasing the type we have

3. Consider sharing a story about how life insurance made a significant impact on the life of a family.

4. Long-Term Care
   A. Define long-term care
   B. How much does a policy cost?
   C. Is it only for very old people in nursing homes?
   D. How does long-term care insurance work?
      1. What are the benefits?
      2. How long do they last?
      3. How does it pay care providers?
   E. Does the U.S. government pay for care?
   F. Who pays if I don't have enough money?
   G. Actions we've taken to prepare for eventuality of a nursing home stay or need for in-home care
   H. Our preferences and desires regarding nursing home and/or in-home care

Recommendation: Invite your insurance agent to discuss various types of insurance, review your current coverages and answer questions about your policies.

Debt and Borrowing Money

1. What is debt?

2. What are the various types of debt?
   A. How does interest vary by type of debt?
   B. What does it take to qualify?
   C. When and how is debt paid back?

3. What organizations loan money?

4. What is a credit score?

5. How do credit/debit cards work?

6. Incurring debt
   A. When might it make sense to incur debt?
   B. When can it be a poor choice to incur debt?

7. Basic rules of borrowing

8. Our view of debt

A. How we have used credit to our advantage during our lives or careers

B. Pitfalls we want to help our children avoid

Recommendation: Share with your children why you feel the way you do about personal debt. This conversation is a great way to pass on your personal values.

Budgeting and Personal Financial Statements

1. Family/Household Budgets
   A. Provide an example (or several).
   B. How are they used most effectively?

2. Personal Financial Statements
   A. Provide an example (or several).
   B. When does one need one?

3. Our tips to make maintaining a family budget and personal financial statement fun
   A. Make it a game.
   B. Build in rewards to celebrate success.

4. How we have used budgeting, saving and investing

Recommendation: If you believe that living within your means and delaying gratification bring their own rewards, talking about budgets presents a great opportunity to communicate that to your children.

Banking

1. Checking accounts
   A. Writing checks
   B. Balancing the account
   C. Online banking
   D. Tying checking account to budget and financial statement
   E. Automatic transfers to savings
   F. Overdrafts

2. Savings accounts
   ~ FDIC insurance

3. Titling bank accounts

    A. Joint vs. single
    B. Impact of divorce

4. Credit cards
    A. Use
    B. Advantages / disadvantages
    C. Impact of divorce

5. An Emergency Fund
    A. Importance / use
    B. Size
    C. Location

6. Safe deposit boxes
    A. Use
    B. Authorized renters
    C. Access at death
    D. Our use, keys, contents

Recommendation: If you have a strong relationship with your personal banker, consider inviting them to address your family on these topics and to tell your children what banking relationships you have established.

Electronic Passwords

1. Secure storage

2. Protection
    ~ Access to trusted persons

3. What happens upon death or incompetence?

4. Our passwords
    A. Where they are located
    B. When we feel it is an appropriate time for children to access them

5. Children's passwords
    ~ What steps have they taken to protect their passwords?

Recommendation: You can likely handle this topic yourself. Alternatively, consider asking your children for advice!

Investing

1. Money managers
   A. What they do
   B. Methods of compensation

2. Asset allocation / diversification

3. Mutual funds

4. Index funds

5. Time horizon

6. Risk tolerance

7. Taxation

8. Our philosophy

Recommendation: This is a topic that may best be served in "bite sizes." Consider asking your investment manager to address the group if he or she is able to speak in layman's terms!

It is critical to find a good communicator that can explain the fundamental principles of investing without losing the audience in technical jargon. Using specific examples can personalize the topic.

Estate Planning

1. Mechanisms of passing assets at death
   A. Wills
   B. Trusts (see above)
   C. Beneficiary designations
   D. Titling of assets

2. What happens when someone dies without a will?

3. How are assets taxed upon death?

4. Who pays taxes at our deaths?

5. Estate Plans
   A. How often should one update their estate plan?

B. Describe your estate plan in as much detail as is comfortable for you.

Recommendation: This topic is best discussed in small parts and should be regularly revisited. The more personalized the examples, the more meaningful the education will be.

Entity Planning

1. Limited liability companies
   A. Function
   B. Use in context of estate planning
   C. Governance (meetings, minutes, leadership, voting rights, etc.)

2. Family partnerships
   A. Function
   B. Use in context of estate planning
   C. Governance (meetings, minutes, leadership, voting rights, etc.)

3. S Corporations
   A. Function
   B. Use in context of estate planning
   C. Governance (meetings, minutes, leadership, voting rights, etc.)

Recommendation: Your attorney is probably best suited to address family members on this complex topic.

Charitable Giving

Most people, even children, are familiar with giving to others in need. Some of your children may not be familiar with some of the techniques and tools of charitable giving.

1. Tax implications

2. Donor advised funds

3. Gifts of assets in lieu of cash

4. Foundations

5. Pledges

6. Split-interest gifts

Recommendation: This is a fertile topic for family meetings and best learned by actual giving. Your children are likely interested in hearing why you give to the causes you've chosen.

CHAPTER 6

Building A Personal
Board Of Advisors

If you have knowledge, let others light their candles with it.
WINSTON CHURCHILL

I f you are reading this book, there is a very good chance you have been financially successful in your lifetime. As I said at the outset, this book is intended for those who have "surplus" and wish to be intentional about deploying that surplus in their estate plans.

With wealth comes complexity. To accumulate, preserve and distribute your wealth most effectively, virtually everyone needs the help of professional experts. Our tax structure, regulatory environment and legal system are too complex to master on our own.

For that reason, we use the services of attorneys, accountants, insurance professionals, investment managers and others to help us navigate the complexity.

During our working careers, we access these advisors on an as-needed basis. While we may see our accountant annually to prepare our tax return, it is not unusual for us to see our attorney only every few years. Our investment advisor may reach out to us a couple of times each year, but we may see our insurance agent

To accumulate, preserve and distribute your wealth...everyone needs the help of professional experts.

only when we have a claim. For the most part, advisors are reactive. When there is a fire they are there to put it out. Until that time, they sit in their firehouses waiting for us to call.

I have worked with professional advisors for over 30 years, sitting through hundreds of client meetings with one or more advisors. I have been privileged to work with some extraordinarily gifted advisors who are committed to providing their clients exemplary service. But, regardless of how bright and committed advisors are, unless they stay abreast of their clients' changing circumstances, and have accurate, comprehensive, timely information from their clients, they cannot deliver the best advice.

Think about it for a moment. An accountant must have records of all of your income and expenses to file accurate tax returns. Your attorney cannot structure the most appropriate estate plan without knowing the type, amount and ownership of your assets, the number and names of your beneficiaries, or the state laws that apply. Without your medical records and the nature of the financial contingency you are trying to insure, your life insurance agent cannot identify the best policy to achieve your goals, much less find a carrier to write it. How can your investment advisor invest your money without understanding your investment time horizon and knowing the amount and reliability of your cash flow, the amount of money you have saved and your tolerance for risk? The more information a professional advisor has about you, the better is the advice they can give.

As we transition from our income-earning years to retirement years, it is important to have a comprehensive plan for coordinating our investments, tax planning, insurance, estate planning, banking and sources of retirement income. Providing detailed, accurate and timely information to our advisors in each of these areas is essential in creating that comprehensive plan. I have found that when we provide advisors all of the information at the same time, far less is lost in translation. Advisors are able ask for clarification and further explanation. There's huge benefit in all advisors sharing in that discussion.

The activities that affect your financial security (spending, distributions to children, donations to charity) are integrally intertwined. Any error in calculating or implementing these actions can significantly affect your comprehensive plan for your retirement years.

Many Cooks Make The Broth Richer.

How you relate (or don't) to your professional advisors can impact your sense of financial security as you transition to the next phase of your life. Of course, receiving conflicting advice from advisors who don't communicate with each other can be confusing and contribute to a sense of insecurity. Unfortunately it happens all too often.

Using advisors as "firefighters" as you prepare for retirement no longer serves you well. While you have never been through retirement, they have helped dozens of individuals navigate the same waters you are about to dive into. They know the questions to ask. They are familiar with the most common emotional reefs that can sink your retirement ship on its retirement voyage.

...if you engage your advisors to meet as a board with you and your spouse, the additional professional fees you may incur will be more than made up in other savings.

While this may seem counter-intuitive, I believe that if you engage your advisors to meet *as a board* with you and your spouse, the additional professional fees you may incur will be more than made up in other savings. The real value, however, will be peace of mind. When you communicate your goals and aspirations directly to all of your advisors, everyone "is on the same page." By exchanging information during the planning process, each advisor can add valuable insight and help you to sail successfully through the next phase of your life.

WHO SHOULD BE ON MY PERSONAL BOARD OF ADVISORS?[3]

Your specific needs dictate which professional advisors you will ask to be members of your Personal Board of Advisors. Typically, a board consists of an estate planning attorney and a tax accountant. A "financial services" professional is typically asked to provide advice on: insurance, investments, Social Security, Medicare, etc. Sometimes a trust officer or a charitable consultant is on a board as well. However, each couple, each family and each situation is unique. Personalities, relationships and your level of financial expertise affect the makeup of your Board. Your most trusted advisor may be your financial planner and you may bring in your accountant and attorney only on an as-needed basis. You decide who sits on your Board.

Too many board members, however, is simply unwieldy. Typically, I would suggest two to three "core" members. There can also be a group of "virtual" board members that are called on only when needed. This group might include: a home and auto insurance agent, property or farm manager, investment specialist, banker, or aging life care consultant. These advisors may be invited to your Board meetings periodically to report to you and your core Board members.

How Do I Choose The Members Of My Board?

Most clients near retirement age have long-standing relationships with one or more professional advisors. Normally this is good. Working with someone you trust and with whom you have a personal relationship makes the process far more enjoyable. (This assumes they are qualified to help you in this phase of your financial life.)

If your best friend is a divorce attorney, that's great. But you need estate planning advice. Ask your divorce attorney friend to refer you to an estate planning specialist.

The same principle holds true for your other advisors. You want and need people who provide specialized knowledge. The most tried-and-true method of finding these people is by referral from other professional advisors.

---

[3] *The estate planning community has recognized the value of collaboration among professional advisors in the estate planning process. Todd Fithian, Albert Gibbons and David Holaday have written a great article in Trusts & Estates magazine (High Performance Teaming and Professional Collaboration). The National Association of Estate Planners & Councils published a White Paper that contains an in-depth examination of collaboration among advisors. I believe collaboration is important during the creation of an estate plan but it is essential in creating a "life plan" for your retirement years if you are to have (and maintain) confidence that you are on track to reaching your goals.*

If you have a solid team of competent professional advisors who know you well and in whom you have confidence, terrific! Keep them and introduce them to the concept of a Personal Board of Advisors. I believe you are typically best served by using advisors you have worked with for many years. However, what if you haven't used advisors much in the past? Or the ones you used have retired or died? How do you go about building the team that will help you create your own Legacy Plan?

The first step is to determine what skills these advisors must have to work with you, to work together and to create the type of plan you want. If you are filling just one or two positions on your Board, think about the personalities and strengths of the existing members and work to fill the gaps.

Once you know what expertise you are looking for, start asking for referrals. I've found that the best way to find high-quality advisors is to ask other high-quality advisors. The best like to work with the best.

To evaluate your existing advisors or prospective advisors, you might consider whether they possess the qualities necessary to work as a team. I've created a checklist to help you to assess prospective board members in the Appendix.

Playing Nice In The Sandbox

Keep in mind that advisors are used to working one-on-one with clients. When they do interact with other advisors, it is typically only for a short duration and on a strictly defined project. There is almost always a "lead" advisor on a project with the others offering ancillary support.

It is quite normal for each advisor to want to display their competence to clients with the idea of assuming the position of predominance. When selecting the members for your Board of Advisors, it is important to choose advisors who truly are "team players." If it becomes obvious that they are "lone wolves" and simply can't adapt to a team environment, you will need to replace them.

THE ADVISOR INVITATION LETTER

To create a Personal Board of Advisors, you must spell out your expectations clearly. The easiest way to do that is to create an Advisor Invitation. I've provided an example in the Appendix. In your invitation, you summarize the purpose of your Board, name the other members and expressly give your permission to share, with the other advisors on your Board, confidential information they may have about you. You may name the person who will act as your Meeting Facilitator or put that choice as an agenda item for your first meeting. Finally, you tell your advisors that you'd like to meet at least annually on an ongoing basis and how you'd like them to bill you for their time.

Think About Succession.

It's quite common that our most trusted advisors are often people we've dealt with for many years. Frequently they are close to our own age. If you are 65 years old and your estate planning attorney is approximately the same age, it is very likely your attorney will have retired by the time you die and your estate is probated. Does that mean you should replace your long-time attorney with a 35-year-old attorney? No. You may be very comfortable with your contemporary and value the experience and wisdom that only comes with age.

I believe the best result is to have the older advisor bring along a young associate to become familiar with your situation. That way, when your primary attorney retires, you won't have to start all over with a new relationship. Will this likely cost you more? Probably, but that is a small price to pay for the comfort of having a built-in succession plan for your key advisors.

WHO LEADS THE BOARD?

You are the chairman of your Board. You set its vision, but it is essential that you choose one person take charge of:
- **Scheduling** meetings
- **Setting** agendas
- **Selecting** the location
- **Taking** notes/minutes

· **Following through** on action items.

This point person is also responsible for communicating with all other advisors and stakeholders.

Your point person is not necessarily the smartest, oldest or most dominant person in the room. Ideally he or she is a "servant leader:" someone who is confident enough in themselves to be happy facilitating and moderating meetings that draw out the best from everyone in the room. Depending on the topic, different advisors may assume the dominant role. Your point person makes certain that everyone has an opportunity to contribute, then helps focus the discussion on creating action items. A good servant leader builds trust between you and your Board and among members of your Board so that everyone is comfortable making suggestions, asking questions, expressing alternative opinions and airing concerns.

How Often Does Your Board Meet?

Once you are at or near retirement, I believe your Personal Board of Advisors should meet with you at least annually and initially, more frequently. Let me explain why I say at least annually by way of a story.

A Husband's Wish Becomes His Widow's Peace Of Mind

Nearly 15 years ago, "Jake" was dying of cancer. While he had been financially successful during his life, his wife of over 40 years ("Agnes") knew very little about their personal finances. Jake was justifiably concerned for Agnes's financial well-being. Shortly before he died, we were reviewing his life insurance program when he put his feeble hand on my arm and said, "Mark, promise me you will always look after my wife." Making a promise to a dying man is something I don't take lightly!

Following Jake's death, I met with Agnes and asked her about her relationship with their advisors. She said that Jake had used both the attorney and accountant for over ten years. While their primary relationship was with Jake, Agnes liked both of them and trusted them. I asked her to introduce me and tell them I wanted to "interview" them.

Once Agnes made the introductions I met separately with each advisor, explained that I wanted to form a "Board of Advisors" and suggested that we meet regularly with Agnes. While initially a bit skeptical, they agreed.

We began meeting quarterly. I brought in a professional money manager to serve on the Board. My staff and I prepared the agenda and took minutes. The Board reviewed all aspects of her financial life including: budgeting, cash management, banking, estate planning, insurance (life, homeowners, automobile, liability), property management, investment management, income taxation, charitable planning, educating her grandchildren, Social Security, Medicare, bill paying and communicating with her adult children. Each meeting lasted 90 minutes to two hours.

Occasionally, Agnes would be approached by a vendor of some sort or asked for a sizable charitable gift. She would bring each request to her Board of Advisors. We would analyze that request in the context of her overall plan, then Agnes would make her decision.

Agnes was afraid of "making a dumb decision" or being "taken advantage of." Having her own Board as a filter provided Agnes great confidence she was making sound decisions. (It also gave her a great excuse to say "no" when friends or family asked for a loan or handout!)

After nearly 15 years of quarterly meetings, we were running out of things to talk about. Agnes had followed all of our recommendations. She had transferred significant assets to her children (but retained lifetime control). She had provided for her grandchildren's education. She had made significant charitable gifts to causes dear to her. Her estate plan was totally up-to-date. Her investments were diversified and performing well. In short, Agnes was in "maintenance mode."

When I suggested we cut back to just semi-annual meetings, Agnes looked me straight in the eye and asked, "Mark, do you know what the most frequent topic is when I have lunch with other widows my age?" I admitted that I had no clue. "Money!" she said. "We all live in fear that we could run out of money one day and be dependent on our children or destitute the next day." Before I could object, she continued, "I know intellectually that I have plenty of money, but emotionally, I occasionally still get worried. Those worries disappear every time we meet. I walk out reassured, grateful and confident." She added, "Mark, I don't care about the fees. I consider them to be an 'insurance premium' for my feeling of financial security. Your fees are a small price to pay for knowing, really knowing, that whatever happens, whether I become incompetent, or even if I die, everything will be take care of. You give me peace of mind."

With Agnes's speech the light bulb popped on in my mind! When we get to retirement age, most of us continue to use professional advisors in the same way we did before we retired. We wait until we have a "problem," then we call an advisor to "fix" it. As advisors we act in nearly the same way: We react like "firemen." We wait until there's a fire and we put it out!

Maybe reacting works for us when we are younger, well connected, at the top of our games and have plenty of time to recover from our mistakes. But as we age, our worlds become smaller. Our bodies begin to fail us. Our memories aren't as sharp as they once were. Our friends lose their health and an alarming number die. We hear tragic stories about people who thought they were financially secure running out of money. We lose power and influence. We naturally become more fearful.

I'm not suggesting that quarterly meetings with your entire Board are necessary, or even appropriate, in every situation. Typically, there may be several meetings during the first year to provide every board member with all of the data, review the current situation, update documents and develop a plan. Thereafter, the frequency of meetings can decrease. However, even when you are in "maintenance mode," I recommend that you meet with your primary advisors at least annually. That's a plan that, in my experience has paid huge emotional and financial dividends to many, many individuals.

How much would we pay to be regularly assured that we are financially secure? How much is it worth to us to know that a team of trusted advisors is looking out for us if we are scammed, or our identity is stolen or if our investments take a dramatic drop?

As a professional advisor, I know how much more effective I am when I see the entire picture of a client's financial affairs and really understand a client's goals and fears. Only then can I use my years of experience to anticipate the client's needs and collaborate with their other advisors to develop and communicate the very best course of action for that client.

Sharing the big picture with advisors and asking—no requiring!—them to work together gives you, in essence, your own Board of Advisors. You can expect your Board to anticipate your needs, protect you from potential predators, but most importantly give you peace of mind.

Conflicts Of Interest

There has been a metamorphosis in the financial services business in recent years. The focus has shifted from referring to other advisors to capturing more revenue from each client relationship.

For example, investment advisors now sell life insurance. Life insurance agents often sell investments. Accountants often sell insurance and investments. Large banks try to do it all. In addition to traditional banking, the bank may invest your money; sell you life insurance; sell you auto, homeowners, annuities, long-term care insurance as well as provide limited legal and accounting services. In short, they want to be a one-stop shop for your financial needs.

From the service provider's perspective, I understand the desire to increase the "revenue per client." It makes economic sense. However, from the client's perspective, I am not convinced.

I've yet to meet an organization that provided "best-in-class" service in all the different aspects of retirement planning. You want each member of your Board to be the very best in their respective fields and focused exclusively on serving you.

Having different advisors from unrelated firms can, at times, be a bit more cumbersome and complex in coordinating schedules than is working with one person who can "do it all." However, the perspective you gain from hearing multiple (and often differing) opinions can be very healthy and often results in the very best decision for you and your family.

WHAT DOES IT COST TO MEET REGULARLY WITH A PERSONAL BOARD OF ADVISORS?

Cost is and always will be a factor in working with a Board of Advisors. No one wants to pay unnecessary professional fees. The amount of fees you pay depends on many factors including: the complexity of your situation, the area of the country you live in, how frequently you meet with your Board, etc. Normally, you incur the heaviest fees up front when your advisors are performing their initial analysis and creating the estate planning documents. Thereafter, fees typically level out.

As an example, let's assume that your Board of Advisors consists of an estate planning attorney, a tax accountant and a financial planner. The attorney and accountant are paid on an hourly basis. The financial planner may charge a fee or alternatively be compensated for investing money and/or receive commissions on insurance products. Fee structure is something you should openly discuss up front.

Assume that, after the initial year of intense planning, your Board meets semi-annually. Each meeting lasts two hours. Assume each advisor on your Board spends an additional two hours preparing for each meeting or following through on action items. In a year's time, that would amount to approximately 24 hours (three advisors x four hours x two meetings). Assume an average hourly rate of $500. That would equate to $12,000 (much of which may be tax deductible).

Ideally, your advisors will move away from billing for each minute of time and evolve toward a meeting fee that resembles the ones used by companies and their boards of directors. Your point person can help advisors move in this direction as it is liberating for them and much more comfortable (and easier to budget!) for you.

I submit that a well-run Personal Board of Advisors can save you tens of thousands and even millions of dollars in income and estate taxes. Aside from the hard dollars saved, peace of mind from having your Personal Board of Advisors meet with you as a team semi-annually is well worth the fees you pay!

A BENEFIT TO WIDOWS

In practical terms, having both spouses work with a Board of Advisors provides great benefit to women since:

· Nearly 1,000,000 women become widows every year.[4]

· Women are four times more likely than men to outlive their spouses.[5]

· Eighty percent of men die married and 80% of women die single.[6]

Having both spouses meet one to two times per year with a Personal Board of Advisors has the potential to create a level of trust between each spouse and those advisors. Regardless of which spouse dies first (or becomes incompetent) the survivor can feel assured he or she is in good hands. Advisors (or their designated successors) will be there to help surviving spouses implement the plans they made when their spouses were alive.

YOUR PARADIGM SHIFT

This chapter is titled "Building a Personal Board of Advisors" for a specific reason: it is meant to be a paradigm shift for both you and your advisors. You have used professional advisors throughout your working career. At times, you may have even asked them to collaborate as a team on a specific project (e.g. the sale of a business, the creation of an estate plan). Once the project was complete, the team dissolved and returned to "on call" status.

---

[4] *U.S. Census Bureau, August 2011, Marital Events of Americans: 2009 (American Community Survey)*

[5] *Widows and Widowhood, Women's Institute For A Secure Retirement,*
http://www.wiserwomen.org/blog/?m=201507#_ednref1

[6] *Five Money Myths That Get Smart Women In Trouble, Women's Institute For A Secure Retirement.*
http://www.wiserwomen.org/index.php?id=184&page=five-money-myths

I am challenging you to think of yourself (and your family) as a company and your professional advisors as a board of directors. Boards hold scheduled meetings at least once or twice per year. They work from prepared agendas and are expected to arrive at meetings prepared to offer insights and suggestions to help the company achieve its goals. Normally, board members are compensated on a fee-per-meeting basis. As Chairman of the Board, you set the vision for your company and oversee board meetings.

I am challenging you to think of yourself (and your family) as a company and your professional advisors as a board of directors.

Putting your attorney, accountant, financial planner and/or other advisors in the role of board members will change both your mindset and theirs. No longer are you expecting only reactions, but proactive suggestions. No longer are they firefighters extinguishing fires. You expect them to anticipate your concerns and provide information before you need it to maintain confidence in your comprehensive plan for retirement. You expect them to offer more than strictly financial and legal advice as they share their insights into the emotional, physical and spiritual issues that you may encounter as you enter this new phase of your life.

Having a Personal Board of Advisors can be incredibly empowering. It can provide confidence that you are, and will remain, financially secure. It can allow you to focus on leaving a legacy of both financial assets and values to your children and community.

In the following chapter, we see how one family used its Board of Advisors to make the transition from working career to retirement with confidence.

Where Are You On The Spectrum Of Building A Personal Board Of Advisors?

Please place a checkmark next to the paragraph that most closely reflects how you currently interact with your professional advisors.

1. _____ We don't use advisors. We haven't updated our wills. We prepare our own tax returns.

2. _____ We have an accountant who prepares our tax returns each year. The only time we call an attorney is if we have a problem. The same is true of our insurance agent. We self-manage our investments.

3. _____ We have used the same attorney, accountant, insurance agent and money manager for a number of years. We don't think they know each other. We just call one of them when we need something.

4. _____ When we updated our estate plan, our insurance professional and attorney met with us. They know who our other advisors are if they need anything from them.

5. _____ We have a comprehensive Legacy Plan that our attorney, accountant and financial advisor prepared together. We communicate with this group throughout the year and meet at least annually to make certain that we remain on track to reach our goals.

Your answer above indicates where you are on a spectrum of possible actions related to creating a personal Board of Advisors. To calculate your progress toward your own Legacy Plan, move your answer to the worksheet at the end of Chapter 8.

CHAPTER 7

One Family's Legacy Plan

Caring about the happiness of others, we find our own.
PLATO

The following case study shows how one fictional family (the Nearys) implemented many of the principles and practices described in this book. Through creating a Legacy Plan and monitoring it regularly, "John and Jane Neary" were able to retire, confident that they were prepared for the next phase of their lives and could nimbly adapt to any event.

In the paragraphs that follow, you'll see how the couple made an in-depth assessment of their financial situation as they approached retirement. In that process, they raised three important questions:

1. How do we know if we have "enough" to be financial secure?

2. How much is enough, but not too much, for our children?

3. How do we leave a legacy to our children and community?

THE NEARY FAMILY CASE STUDY

Some Background

John and Jane Neary both recently turned 65. They were college sweethearts and have been married for 40 years. They have three children: Jennifer (38), Nancy (36) and Alex (35). All are married. Combined, the Nearys have 10 grandchildren. While the children all live within a 300-mile radius of John and Jane, none lives in the same town. John, Jane and the children remain emotionally close, however, as the children have grown, the demands of daily life in their young families mean John and Jane see them less frequently than they'd like.

John is the founder and sole owner of Neary & Associates, a successful architectural firm, employing a dozen architects with expertise in building health-care-related facilities. Jane retired last year after teaching American history for nearly 25 years at the state university. She finally has the time to pursue her passion to travel the United States in search of historically significant quilts. Jane has never been very interested in John's business or family finances, and has been content to rely entirely on John's judgment.

As Jane was nearing the end of her teaching career, John developed his own business succession plan. In it, he agreed to sell all of his interest in the firm to his two junior partners at the end of five years. During that time, he would take a fixed salary and gradually transfer his clients to his partners. He would take more time off to travel with Jane before retiring completely at the end of that five-year period.

Jane's parents died years ago, as did John's father, but his mother died only a year ago after an extended stay in a nursing home. As an only child and executor of his mother's estate, John experienced, first hand, the complexities of the estate settlement process. He is committed to having all of his financial affairs in order for Jane and their children. Now that he has more time away from the office, he has turned his attention to developing a comprehensive retirement/estate plan.

The Nearys' Prior Financial Planning

About 10 years ago, John and Jane began working with Allen, a local (and highly recommended) financial planner. Allen helped the couple to arrange their finances so they could both retire at age 65, if they chose to do so. Some of the action items Allen implemented included:

- **Helped** John and Jane develop and follow a family budget.
- **Showed** the Nearys how to pay off all debt by age 62.
- **Helped** the couple to maximize their retirement savings from a variety of sources.
- **Developed** an investment strategy using a diversified portfolio of mutual funds.

- **Introduced** John and Jane to Curt, an estate planning attorney, who implemented an estate plan that provided maximum financial security and flexibility to the surviving spouse and distributed any remaining balance to children and charity.

- **Established** two irrevocable trusts funded by life insurance. The first trust holds a $1,000,000 variable life policy on John's life for the benefit of Jane. The second trust holds a $3,000,000 variable second-to-die policy on the lives of John and Jane for the benefit of their children and grandchildren. Using an inheritance received from their parents, the Nearys pre-funded the insurance trusts so no premiums would be required after retirement.

- **Increased** their personal umbrella liability policy to help protect the assets they had accumulated for their retirement from potential lawsuits.

- **Purchased** long-term care insurance policies (with generous Cost of Living Riders) on each John and Jane. All premiums were paid up when they reached age 65.

- **Funded** a donor-advised fund at their community foundation with $500,000 of highly appreciated securities to pre-fund the couple's charitable contributions during their retirement years in anticipation of lower spendable income.

All in all, John and Jane felt quite good about working with Allen over the last ten years. They met with him annually and he almost always had suggestions to improve their financial plan. If I had asked John and Jane to indicate where they were on the Financial Security Spectrum at the end of Chapter Two, they would have looked for the option indicating that they'd done everything possible.

The Chartered Advisor In Philanthropy® Study Group Experience Changes Everything

Slightly over a year ago, both Allen and Curt were invited to participate in a study group at their community foundation to achieve their Chartered Advisor in Philanthropy® (CAP®) designation. While they each felt that, individually, they'd provided sound financial advice for their mutual client (John and Jane), the CAP® process made them realize there was much work they could still do for the Nearys. Together, they approached Jane and John, shared what they learned in the CAP® program and proposed that the Nearys take the next step in a collaborative planning process. John and Jane readily agreed. With Jane having retired and John slowing down, they now had the time and motivation to do more comprehensive planning.

Allen and Curt scheduled an extended meeting with John and Jane in their home, and described what they'd learned in CAP® class about "Above the Line" and "Below the Line" planning.[7] They had been doing Below-the-Line planning (The "How") with their clients for years. They were now excited to incorporate Above-the-Line planning (The "Why") with their best clients.

The meeting with the Nearys lasted the entire afternoon. Through open-ended, probing questions, combined with the patience to actively listen, Allen and Curt were able to elicit the Nearys' story. John and Jane acknowledged that they felt they had accumulated more wealth than they needed for their own financial security, but that questions had begun to creep into their minds as the end of their working careers neared. Some of their questions were:

1. How do we know if we have "enough" to be financially secure?

The Nearys had heard many stories of people running out of money in their later years and becoming dependent on family or the government for survival. While the Nearys felt they had more than most people they knew, they had some lingering doubts.

2. How much is enough, but not too much, for our children?

Their children were doing fine, and John and Jane were proud of them, but they had seen first-hand what too much money, received suddenly, could do to families. From an early age the Nearys had

---

[7] *In the insightful book,* The Right Side of the Table, *authors Scott and Todd Fithian describe "The Planning Horizon." Below the horizon are the "How" questions and above it are the "Why" questions. Most professionals are most comfortable operating below the horizon. Those conversations deal with tactics, strategies, products and taxes. Above-the-line conversations deal with why you want to provide for your children, why you worry that your money could do them more harm than good and why you want to give to a cause you are passionate about. Students in the CAP classes learn how to listen with a discerning ear in order to fully understand why a person feels the way they do. Only then do they work with other advisors on how to accomplish an individual's dreams and aspirations.*

drilled into their children the importance of self-sufficiency. John and Jane firmly believed that the sense of self-worth that one achieved by "making it on their own" was far more rewarding than receiving a large sum of money one didn't work for. This made them wonder:

· How much should they give their children?

· Once they decide on the appropriate amount, should they give money to their children while alive to watch them use the assets or leave them cash after they both pass away?

· And if they decide to give their children money after they die, should the inheritance be in one lump sump or put in trust?

If they died today, the Nearys' existing estate planning documents distributed their assets to their children when each child turned 40. Now that their three children approached this age, they weren't so sure that they wanted their children to receive their one-third share of the estate outright at age 40. The Nearys told Allen and Curt that they wanted to think through these issues.

3. How can we leave a legacy to our children and our community?

The Nearys had both been involved, and continued to be involved, with several charitable organizations. They regularly donated to these organizations, but they wanted to make more significant gifts upon their deaths. They just weren't sure how much they could afford to commit.

· How much would they spend during retirement?

· How much should they leave their children without doing more harm than good?

If there were a way to figure this all out and be confident there would be enough money, they'd be excited to see such a plan come together. They also wanted to feel assured that their children would be good stewards of any money they inherited.

THE NEARYS ANSWER THE THREE QUESTIONS

The Nearys' planning was focused on the three primary questions:

1. How do we know if we have "enough" to be financial secure?

2. How much is enough, but not too much, for our children?

3. How do we leave a legacy to our children and community?

Question 1: How do we know if we have "enough" to be financially secure during our retirement years?

The following are the planning assumptions and financial spreadsheets that the Nearys' advisors prepared for them to help the Nearys become confident that they could meet their financial goals.

· Legacy Planning Assumptions

· Personal Financial Statement

· Budget Worksheet

· Cash Flow Summary

· Family Legacy Plan Balance Sheet Summary

· What If? Worksheet

Summary: By working through as many contingencies as possible, minimizing expenses during retirement years, building in conservative assumptions about investment results and income needed, and meeting regularly with their Personal Board of Advisors, John and Jane became confident that they could live comfortably during their retirement years.

Question 2: How much is enough, but not too much, for our children?

To determine how much money to leave their children, the Nearys completed worksheets that organized their thinking and initiated dialogue between themselves and between them and their advisors. They then wrote letters to their children and trustees to communicate their intentions and, they hoped, avoid or minimize misunderstandings.

· Why We Choose To Leave Money To Our Children
· The Legacy Worksheet
· How We Chose Our Inheritance Amount
· How We Would Like Our Children To Use Their Inheritance
· Legacy Letter To The Neary Children
· Neary Letter To Trustee

Summary: John and Jane decided to leave each of their three children up to a maximum of $3,000,000 each, indexed to inflation to preserve its spending power. This amount would be left to their children only if John and Jane did not need the money for their own retirement needs. This amount was considerably more than they had initially planned to leave, but Jane and John felt good about the increased amount because they had put in place both appropriate safeguards and a plan to educate their children about financial matters. The children would receive ten percent outright in a lump sum. The balance (90%) would be put in a generation-skipping trust for the benefit of their children and their heirs. The children could ask to be named trustee over their trust portion upon turning age 40 subject to the approval of a trustee. Children who felt that they did not "need" the money could leave it in trust for their children and future grandchildren, free of estate tax.

The Nearys' advisors worked with them to prepare letters conveying their wishes to the trustees and the children. They also agreed to help the Nearys develop agendas for their family meetings designed to pass on their values and information about personal finances. With trust arrangements and an educational plan in place, John and Jane felt comfortable with the inheritance amount they would leave for each child. Still, they wanted maximum flexibility so reserved the right to change the amount left to their children and charitable institutions if they so desired. They directed their advisors to draft all documents with maximum flexibility, including "escape clauses" whenever possible. With the exception of some irrevocable gifts to fund insurance premiums and college costs, John and Jane retained lifetime control of all other assets.

Question 3: How do we leave a legacy to our children and community?

Leaving a legacy that included not only financial assets to their children and community, but also passed their personal values to their children were essential parts of the Nearys' Legacy Plan. To accomplish that, the Nearys completed the following worksheets:

· The Values We Hope To Pass On

· Invitation To Children To Family Meetings

· Invitation To Join Personal Board Of Advisors

· Post-Death Philanthropy Plan

· Statement Of Intent: Neary Family Educational Trust

Forming a Personal Board of Advisors was an essential part of executing John and Jane's Legacy Plan. Their Board gave the Nearys great confidence that their wishes would be carried out. To explain the role they were asking their advisors to play, the Nearys sent a letter of invitation to their advisors.

Summary: Through a comprehensive plan, reasonable financial projections and the support of a Personal Board of Advisors charged with monitoring the plan, John and Jane gained the assurance they sought that there would be sufficient money left over upon their deaths to leave their children a generous inheritance. Furthermore, they make significant bequests to charitable causes dear to them. Holding family meetings would provide a platform for their children to learn to responsibly handle a significant inheritance. Finally, including their children in their charitable giving could create another forum for the family to work together to make the community a better place to live and help carry out John and Jane's personal legacy.

Rome Was Built in A Year, Not A Day

The Nearys completed their plan over the course of a year. It took three Board of Advisor meetings and communication between meetings. The nearly $25,000 that the Nearys paid in professional fees during the first year was certainly more than they normally paid. Still they were very pleased with the result, and content that all the work they had done was a prudent investment.

The Nearys understood that they had initiated an ongoing process. Their intent was to meet with their Board of Advisors twice per year for the first couple of years, but they expected to cut back to annual meetings.

Having implemented their plan, when the Nearys hear the insecurity in the voices of their friends as they discuss retirement, John and Jane are confident in their ability to enjoy a comfortable retirement. As they watch others struggle with how much to leave their children, John and Jane know that the amount they will leave their children and how they will leave it are consistent with their values. They are excited that their Legacy Plan includes growing closer as a family through family meetings and gaining confidence in their children's money management skills.

While they wish they could afford to give more to the few non-profits with which they work closely, they are gratified that one day they will be able to leave them very meaningful charitable bequests.

Lastly, they feel empowered to create their own Personal Board of Advisors. The Nearys like the fact that their Personal Board has helped others through this process. They love that their Board "has their back!" Having regular meetings focused solely on their concerns keeps them on track. They are excited about living their final years free of fear and in a state of abundance.

THE NEARYS' WORK PAPERS

On the following pages are the assumptions and spreadsheets that the Nearys' advisors used to help John and Jane develop confidence that they had enough for their own financial security. Following those spreadsheets are the forms the Nearys used to determine how much they would leave their children and letters to communicate their intentions to their children and trustee.

FORM

Legacy Planning Assumptions

Personal Financial Statement

Budget Worksheet

Cash Flow Summary

Balance Sheet Summary

What If? Worksheet

Why We Choose To Leave Money To Our Children

Legacy Worksheet

How We Chose Our Inheritance Amount

How We Would Like Our Children To Use Their Inheritance

Legacy Plan Letter To Children

Letter To Trustee

The Values We Hope To Pass On

Invitation To Children To Family Meetings

Invitation To Join Our Personal Board Of Advisors

Post-Death Philanthropy Plan

Statement Of Intent: Family Education Trust

Legacy Planning Assumptions
John & Jane Neary

Investment Growth Rate: 6.0%

Retirement Growth Rate: 6.0%

Education Fund Growth Rate: 6.0%

COLA SSI Rate: 2.47%

Inflation Rate: 3.0%

Real Growth: 3.0%

We assumed that:

· Net cash available to invest will be applied to the investment account.

· Personal - Miscellaneous expenses are $10,000 in Year 1 and grow by inflation.

· Expenses related to Insurance Premiums, Business Dues and Contributions will cease at age 70.

· The expense related to Vacation declines beginning at age 75 and ends at age 85.

· Expenses related to Golf Trips and Quilting Trips will increase until 71, decrease from 71 to 85 and cease at 85.

· Expenses attributable to Athletic Events, Golf Club and Health Club will cease at age 85.

· The Nearys have used a portion of their Lifetime Exemptions to fund their life insurance trusts and grandchildren's college education fund.

PERSONAL FINANCIAL STATEMENT
JOHN & JANE NEARY

Date: _____

Assets

Cash - Money Market	$200,000
Emergency Fund	$200,000
Investment Account	$3,500,000
IRA/401(k)s	$2,500,000
Partnerships	$1,000,000
Real Estate	$500,000
Personal Property	$50,000
Total Assets	**$7,950,000**

Liabilities

Credit Cards	$10,000
Total Liabilities	$10,000

Net Worth **$7,940,000**

BUDGET WORKSHEET
JOHN & JANE NEARY

Date: _____

Receipts	Total
Interest	$35,000
Dividends	$72,500
S Corp Distributions	$100,000
W-2 income	$500,000
Total Receipts	**$707,500**

Disbursements	
Food (Groceries, Dining Out)	$25,000
Home (Utilities, Maint., Real Estate Taxes)	$33,300
Income Taxes	$235,000
Automobile (Gas, Maintenance, Taxes)	$15,700
Clothing	$4,000
Gifts	$14,000
Insurance (Life, Disability, Medical)	$57,100
Clubs (Health, Golf)	$8,200
Trips, Vacation	$28,000
Personal Maintenance (Hair, Nails)	$3,000
Entertainment (Sports Events, Movies)	$9,500
Professional Fees	$20,000
Contributions (Charity, Political)	$29,000
401(k) Contributions	$23,000
Business Dues	$2,350
Miscellaneous	$10,000
Total Disbursements	**$517,150**

Net Surplus/Deficit	**$190,350**

CASH FLOW SUMMARY
JOHN & JANE NEARY

	Year 1	Year 6	Year 11	Year 16	Year 21	Year 26
John's Age	65	70	75	80	85	90
Jane's Age	65	70	75	80	85	90
Receipts:						
W-2 Income	500,000					
S Corp Distribution	100,000					
Investment Income	107,500	128,053	152,209	184,066	221,989	268,677
Social Security	-	20,106	45,429	51,324	57,983	65,507
Pension	-	80,000	80,000	80,000	80,000	80,000
IRA Distribution	-	115,419	158,803	206,857	262,315	313,272
Other	-	-	-	-	-	-
Total Receipts	$707,500	$343,579	$437,441	$522,247	$622,288	$727,457
Disbursements:						
Household (utilities, food, etc.)	63,850	74,020	85,809	99,476	115,320	133,688
Insurance (medical, auto, etc.)	62,600	16,376	18,984	22,008	25,513	29,577
Taxes (income, real estate, etc.)	247,000	120,911	140,169	162,495	188,376	218,379
Entertainment (clubs, hobbies, etc.)	25,700	29,793	33,323	35,764	39,000	5,234
Travel / Vacation	20,000	23,185	26,878	35,764	39,000	11,255
Retirement Contributions	23,000	-	-	31,159	36,122	-
Gifts (holiday, wedding, etc.)	14,000	16,230	18,815	21,812	25,286	29,313
Charitable	25,000	-	-	-	-	-
Professional Fees (legal, acctg., etc.)	26,000	23,185	26,878	31,159	36,122	41,876
Personal - Miscellaneous	10,000	11,593	13,439	15,580	18,061	20,938
Total Disbursements	$517,150	$315,294	$364,296	$419,453	$483,800	$490,260
Net Cash Available to Invest/Gift	$190,350	$28,285	$73,146	$102,794	$138,487	$237,197

FAMILY LEGACY PLAN BALANCE SHEET SUMMARY
JOHN & JANE NEARY

	Age	65	70	75	80	85	90
NEARYS' ESTATE	Assumed	Year 1	Year 6	Year 11	Year 16	Year 21	Year 26
Cash / Investments / Real Estate	Growth						
Money Market/Checking Accts.	0.00%	200,000	200,000	200,000	200,000	200,000	200,000
Emergency Fund	0.00%	200,000	200,000	200,000	200,000	200,000	200,000
Investment Account	6.00%	3,500,000	5,669,789	7,891,038	11,032,904	15,419,238	21,766,990
Partnerships	3.00%	1,000,000	1,159,274	1,343,916	1,557,967	1,806,111	2,093,778
Residence & Personal Property	1.00%	550,000	575,505	602,311	630,484	660,095	691,216
IRAs/401(k)s	6.00%	2,500,000	3,353,796	3,695,663	3,891,777	3,848,323	3,461,962
Total Assets Included In Nearys' Estate		**$7,950,000**	**$11,158,364**	**$13,932,929**	**$17,513,134**	**$22,133,767**	**$28,413,947**
Lifetime Exemption	3.00%						
Total Lifetime Exemption		8,830,000	10,236,390	11,866,782	13,756,852	15,947,962	18,488,059
Exemption Over/(Under)		880,000	(921,974)	(2,066,147)	(3,756,281)	(6,185,805)	(9,925,888)
OUT OF NEARYS' ESTATE							
Life Insurance Death Benefit		4,000,000	4,000,000	4,000,000	4,000,000	4,000,000	4,000,000
Education Securities	6.00%						
Education Fund Balance		1,000,000	1,338,226	1,575,723	1,177,307	323,212	-
Disbursements		-	-	(163,394)	(142,064)	(164,691)	-
Total Education Fund Balance		1,000,000	1,338,226	1,412,329	1,035,243	158,520	-
Total Assets Excluded from Nearys' Estate		5,000,000	5,338,226	5,412,329	5,035,243	4,158,520	4,000,000
Total Assets		**$12,950,000**	**$16,496,589**	**$19,345,258**	**$22,548,376**	**$26,292,288**	**$32,413,947**
Present Value of $9,000,000		9,000,000	10,433,467	12,095,247	14,021,707	16,255,001	18,844,001
From ILIT		4,000,000	4,000,000	4,000,000	4,000,000	4,000,000	4,000,000
From Taxable Estate		5,000,000	6,433,467	8,095,247	10,021,707	12,255,001	14,844,001
Excess For Charitable Purposes		2,950,000	4,724,897	5,837,681	7,491,427	9,878,766	13,569,945

WHAT IF? WORKSHEET
JOHN & JANE NEARY

RISK: **What if one (or both) of us needs to go into a nursing home?**

ADVISOR RESPONSES:

You have several sources of income:

1. Long-term care insurance,

2. A sizeable cash reserve, and

3. Your IRA / investment fund.

RISK: **What if we incur huge medical bills?**

ADVISOR RESPONSES:

You have:

1. Medicare and Medicare Supplement policies,

2. A sizeable cash reserve,

3. Your IRA / investment fund, and

4. Long-term care insurance that covers in-home care.

RISK: **What if our children need our financial help?**

ADVISOR RESPONSES:

You have:

1. A sizeable cash reserve for contingencies like these, and

2. Retirement assets from which you can withdraw lump sums.

RISK: **What if we get sued and lose everything?**

ADVISOR RESPONSES:

1. You have a significant personal liability umbrella policy.

2. Your assets are divided between you.

3. Your trusts may provide some additional protection from creditors.

RISK: What if the stock market crashes?

ADVISOR RESPONSES:

1. *Your Personal Board of Advisors can help you navigate rough waters.*

2. *You could draw on your cash reserves until the market recovers.*

3. *Much of your income is unrelated to market fluctuations such as your pension and Social Security payments.*

4. *You have no debt.*

5. *Your current investment assumptions are conservative.*

RISK: What if one of our children divorces?

ADVISOR RESPONSES:

You have:

1. *A sizeable cash reserve for contingencies like these, and*

2. *Retirement assets from which you can withdraw lump sums.*

RISK: What if one of us dies suddenly?

ADVISOR RESPONSES:

1. *You have adequate resources so that the survivor will experience no change in lifestyle.*

2. *Your estate planning documents are up-to-date.*

3. *Members of your Personal Board of Advisors will help the survivor to manage all legal and financial issues.*

RISK: What if we don't have enough money to leave anything to our children or charity?

ADVISOR RESPONSES:

1. *Your plan provides that your children and designated charities receive money only if money remains in your estate when both of you die.*

2. *You have made no commitment to either your children or charity.*

3. *Your financial security is the primary goal of your plan and concern of your Personal Board of Advisors.*

RISK: What if the government significantly raises the federal estate tax?

ADVISOR RESPONSES:

1. *Your Personal Board of Advisors will help you adjust to any changes in tax law.*

2. *Life insurance and your Educational Trust provide some protection from most changes that the IRS is likely to make.*

RISK: What if one of us gets Alzheimer's?

ADVISOR RESPONSES:

1. *Your powers of attorney cover major decisions.*

2. *You have long-term care insurance policies to pay for care.*

3. *Your Personal Board of Advisors will help manage your financial affairs.*

RISK: What if Social Security goes broke?

ADVISOR RESPONSES:

If that would happen:

1. *You have plenty of other assets to make up for any loss of Social Security payments.*

2. *You can reduce the amounts you plan to give to your children and/or charity.*

3. *Your personal Board of Advisors would help you to make any necessary adjustments.*

RISK: What if our identities are stolen and all our accounts are wiped out?

ADVISOR RESPONSES:

1. *You have identity theft "insurance" and will be notified of any change in your credit scores.*

2. *Your banker and investment advisor will immediately alert us to any unusual activity.*

3. *We monitor your financial situation on a regular basis.*

RISK: What if we change our minds about how much we want to leave to our children or to charity?

ADVISOR RESPONSES:

1. *Your plan provides you maximum flexibility to make changes as you wish.*

2. *The plan keeps you in control of your assets until your deaths.*

RISK: What if Curt, Allen or any of our other advisors retire before we die?

ADVISOR RESPONSES:

1. *Because this is likely to happen, each of us has identified a successor within our firms.*

2. *Those successors are familiar with your plan and are prepared to step in immediately to provide ongoing service.*

RISK: What if we change our minds about which charities we want to give to or the amount we want to give?

ADVISOR RESPONSES:

1. *You have made no legal commitment or communicated any gift amounts to any charity.*

2. *You can change your mind at any time without having to notify anyone.*

Curt and Allen encouraged the Nearys to contact them if any new What Ifs? occurred to them between meetings. Not only would the advisors respond immediately, they would add the new What If? to the list. The advisors would discuss the entire list at each meeting to reinforce the Nearys' confidence both in having "enough" and in an advisor team that listened and "had their backs."

Why We Choose To Leave Money To Our Children
John & Jane Neary

Most estate planning presupposes that parents want to leave assets to their children upon their deaths. Leaving assets, however, is a choice. Under the law, you may leave your assets to any individual, institution or entity you choose. If you do not have living children, or choose not to leave them assets upon your death(s), please so indicate below. If you have living children (and/ or grandchildren), however, and you intend to leave a portion of your estate to them, please articulate the three or four specific reasons you have chosen to do so. If you are married, it is important to complete this worksheet together.

Today's Date: <u>MM/DD/YYYY</u>

_____ We do not have living children or do not want our assets to pass to them.

__X__ We want to leave a portion of our wealth to our children for the following reasons. In order of priority those reasons include:

1. *Jane and I dearly love our three children (Jennifer, Nancy and Alex) and want to share with them a portion of any surplus that may be left over upon our deaths.*

2. *We believe that education is critical and want each of our grandchildren to have the opportunity to earn a college degree without incurring debt. Making this money available to our grandchildren and relieving our children from this expense is another gift to our children.*

3. *It is our understanding that we can pass a certain sum of money to our three children upon our deaths without paying estate taxes.*

4. *We want to create a financial safety net for each of our children so that regardless of what setbacks they experience, each may retire with financial security.*

5. _____

_____

Note: This form has no legal binding effect. Your advisors may use it to trigger thought, discussion and dialogue as they work to create a Legacy Plan for you.

LEGACY WORKSHEET
JOHN & JANE NEARY

Before you and your spouse set an inheritance amount that is appropriate for your family, I suggest that you first ask yourselves the following thought-provoking questions about your own situation, your children and your current plan about how to transfer your wealth. Once you have reached a consensus, share your answers with your advisors. Doing so provides them valuable insight and guidance as they create your Legacy Plan.

Today's Date: *MM/DD/YYYY*

Your Situation

1. What is your approximate net worth? *$6 million*

2. What is the nature of your assets (e.g. closely held business, farmland, commercial real estate, life insurance, securities)? *securities, IRAs*

3. How old are you? *65 and 65*

4. What is your estimated life expectancy? *20 to 30 years?*

5. How would you describe your relationship with your children? *Very good*

6. What type of lifestyle do you live? *Comfortable, middle to upper-middle class*

Your Children

1. How old are your children? *35, 36 and 38*

2. Are they all from the same marriage? *Yes*

3. Are they single, married, divorced? *All married (no divorces)*

4. What career paths have they taken? *Teacher, homemaker, banker*

5. What type of lifestyle did your children grow up in? *Fairly meager in the early years. We didn't begin to "have money" until our children were in college.*

6. What level of financial maturity have they exhibited to date? *All seem to be doing well.*

7. How have they handled any significant cash gifts you have given? _We only give them $500 to $1000 at Christmastime and, on occasion, an airline ticket._

8. Are they savers or spenders? _We don't know. Presumably they aren't able to save much yet._

9. Do you meet with your children regularly? _Yes_

Distribution Plans

1. Do you intend to leave an equal amount to each child? **Yes** If not, please explain why. _____

2. Is it your intent to transfer significant assets to your children during your lifetimes or only upon your deaths? _Only at death. We want them to make it on their own._

   A. If at death, will you give to them outright or in trust? _Probably some cash outright, but most in trust._

   B. If in trust, when will your children ultimately receive the assets? _After age 40?_

How We Chose Our Inheritance Amount
John & Jane Neary

Complete this form only after you have completed: "Why We Choose To Leave Money To Our Children" and The Legacy Worksheet.

Today's Date: *MM/DD/YYYY*

1. We believe that today, our combined estates will be worth about
   $12,000,000 upon our deaths.

2. We would like to leave our children an amount of as much as
   $9,000,000 upon our deaths.

You can express this number as a flat amount or as a percentage of your total estate if you prefer. You can include a "not to exceed" instruction with the amount. You can adjust the amount for inflation or state a set, unchanging amount. If you desire, you can state different amounts or percentages for different children or treat all children the same. Use the lines below to describe your intentions.

This amount should be divided equally among our three children and indexed for inflation. We want to give up to this amount, but not more. The amount may be less if we spend more during our retirement than we anticipate, or if we give more to charity. In other words, $9,000,000 (plus the inflation factor) is a "not to exceed" amount.

3. We choose to leave this amount because:
Mark all statements that apply and provide explanations, if appropriate.

X *The amount should be enough to achieve most or all of the items (listed on our "How We Would Like Our Children To Use Their Inheritance" Worksheet) that we'd like to provide for our children.*

X *We think that we will have enough left in our estate at our deaths to provide this amount without affecting our retirement income needs.*

X *We believe that this inheritance amount will not affect our ability to make the charitable bequests we desire.*

__X__ *It is our understanding that we can leave this inheritance to our children without adverse tax consequences.*

__X__ *We (will develop) or (have already developed) a plan to help educate our children on how to handle an inheritance of this size in accordance with our values.*

__X__ *We feel that we can use trusts (or other entities) to protect our children's inheritance from creditors and predators.*

__X__ *We plan to communicate with our children, in writing and in person, about how we want them to use the inheritance they may receive from us. In addition, we intend to revisit our inheritance decision regularly with our advisors. Finally, we are comfortable with this amount ___$9,000,000___ at this time.*

_____ _____

      _____

      _____

John and Jane Neary

Note: While this Worksheet is designed to help you be purposeful in the distribution of your assets upon your death, it has no legal, binding effect. Your advisors will use it to initiate dialogue with you in the development of a Legacy Plan customized to meet your specific goals.

How We Would Like Our Children
To Use Their Inheritance
John & Jane Neary

The purpose of this Worksheet is to help you make decisions about how you want your children to use the money you will leave and communicate your wishes to them. Both spouses should agree on the approximate amounts. While you cannot mandate how your children actually spend the money, this exercise will help you calculate an approximate amount that is comfortable for you. You may also use this Worksheet to clarify and communicate your values to your children at the appropriate time.

Check the items that reflect your intentions and add others as you desire. Use the blank lines to add your thoughts, comments or explanations.

Today's Date: _MM/DD/YYYY_

We would feel good about our children using the inheritance they may receive from us to:

✔ Further their (or their children's) educations.

We believe education is essential to finding self-fulfillment and becoming knowledgeable, contributing members of society. For that reason, we have set aside enough money to pay four years of in-state tuition for our grandchildren. We are fine with our children using their inheritance to pay for graduate schools or private grade or high schools for themselves and our grandchildren.

Range: _$100,000 - $200,000_

✔ Pay off debt.

Paying off existing debt (credit cards, student loans, mortgages) provides financial security. We believe that delaying gratification by making purchases only when you have saved enough to pay with cash is consistent with our values.

Range: _$50,000 - $300,000?_

✔ Be able to retire at normal retirement age and live their final years self-sufficiently.

We want each of our children to retire with dignity. We hope that each child will have approximately $100,000/year in spendable income from all sources. We are happy to supplement their current savings for retirement.

Range: *$1,000,000?*

✔ Purchase a bigger home.

As our children's families grow, we are fine with helping them purchase larger homes (within reason!).

Range: *$250,000 - $500,000?*

✔ Start or acquire a business.

We consider it good use of our money to provide seed money to launch businesses that could allow our children to generate enough money to support themselves.

Range: *$100,000 - $300,000?*

✔ Create an emergency fund.

We'd like each child to have a cash fund for emergencies equal to at least their annual income.

Range: *$50,000 - $200,000?*

NO Purchase a vacation home.

Our interest is in providing personal financial security for our children, not in supporting a lavish lifestyle. Any second homes should be purchased from our children's personal savings.

Range: *$0*

✔ Start an investment fund.

We like the idea of helping our children develop the discipline of saving and learning to invest their savings wisely.

Range: *$100,000*

NO Collect art, jewelry, sports cars, etc.

Our interest is in providing financial security for our children, not in supporting a lavish lifestyle. If children choose to live the "high life" (or "high on the hog") they should do so using their own hard-earned dollars.

Range: *$0*

✔ Help those less fortunate through gifts to charity.

We encourage our children to be generous, but only after they have assured their own financial security. Once they are supporting themselves, we do not mind them using a portion of their inheritance to help others.

Additional comments:

Each of our children will be in a different "financial place" when we die. They will have already paid for many of the items listed here. We don't intend this list to be exhaustive, but do want to describe, with some clarity, the expenditures we feel good about our children making with the inheritance we leave. Our primary goal is that our children be able to retire without money worries and that our grandchildren receive good educations without incurring debt.

Name: *Jane and John Neary*

LEGACY PLAN LETTER TO THE NEARY CHILDREN

MM/DD/YYYY

Dear Jen, Nancy and Alex:

We recently updated our estate planning documents. Although we are in excellent health and hope to live for many years to come, life is unpredictable. While our documents explain "how" our assets are to be distributed, this letter explains "why" we structured our estate plan in the manner we did.

Parents teach their children throughout their lifetimes by both their words and actions. Our estate planning and other documents will be our last "lesson." We want them to reflect our values.

This letter is not a legal document and does not supersede our will or trusts. Where there appears to be inconsistencies, the legal documents control. We write this merely as a means to explain our intent.

In "broad brush" terms, our estate plans leave our assets upon our deaths to each other. Only upon the death of the second spouse will assets pass to you. While you will each receive an equal share, it will be a specific dollar amount (with an inflation provision). The balance will pass to our charitable foundation.

While our parents met all of our needs as children, when we finished our schooling it was made clear we were on our own to make our way in the world. When we had our first child, your mother decided she wanted to stay at home until you all were in school. Since she had a good job and I had just started working, it put a financial strain on us. Business was quite slow in the early years and we had little discretionary income as our family grew. But we had each other. Our friends were in a similar situation and we had fun making do with the little we had. When Alex went off to school, your mother went back to school to get her doctorate. Money was tight when you were young, but we have no regrets. We are very pleased how each of you has turned out.

The primary goal of my estate plan is to make certain your mother has absolute financial security for the remainder of her life. Because I have complete confidence in her judgment, my trust documents provide significant latitude to her while still being tax-efficient and providing protection from creditors and predators.

One of the wonderful gifts our parents gave each of us was a college education. We didn't have a true appreciation of this until we had multiple children in college at the same time. It was only then we realized the financial sacrifice our parents had made.

While we helped you through college, we also want to help your children, our grandchildren. We have set aside a certain sum of money for our grandchildren's college tuition. We do not know how many will go to college or how much college will cost. We feel reasonably confident we have accumulated enough to cover four years of in-state tuition, plus room and board for each grandchild. Your children may take more than four years, may go to private or out-of-state schools. You will still need to save for their schooling. However, we are confident we have provided them a significant head start. (In a separate letter, we have spelled out in more detail the educational fund.)

Perhaps the greatest gift our parents left us was the example of hard work and living within their means. We were given the freedom to fail and the opportunity to make it on our own.

Over the years, we have witnessed the impact of inherited wealth on beneficiaries. Some children are able to handle the wealth wisely. We've found this particularly true if the inherited asset is a family-owned business. However, when the wealth is cash or securities, more often than not, the impact can be detrimental. The recipient often has low self-esteem and tends to over compensate by buying big homes, fancy cars, jewelry, and living an extravagant lifestyle.

The following short story illustrates our point.

One day a man found a butterfly cocoon with a small opening. He sat and watched for hours as the tiny butterfly struggled to force its body through that little hole. Then the butterfly stopped making progress. It appeared as if it could go no further.

So the man decided to help the butterfly. With a pair of scissors, he snipped off the remaining bit of the cocoon. The butterfly then emerged easily, but it had a swollen body and small, shriveled wings.

The man continued to watch the butterfly because he expected that, at any moment, its wings would enlarge and expand and its swollen body would contract.

Neither happened! In fact, the butterfly spent the rest of its short life crawling on the ground with a swollen body and shriveled wings. It never was able to fly.

What the man, in his kindness and haste, did not understand was that the restricting cocoon forced the butterfly to struggle to get through the tiny opening. This design was God's way of forcing the fluid from the body of the butterfly into its wings so that the butterfly could fly once it freed itself from the cocoon.

Sometimes struggles are exactly what we need to be successful in our lives. If God allowed us to go through our lives without any obstacles, we would never reach our full potential. We would not be as strong as we are after overcoming challenges. Without struggle we cannot fly!

On many occasions we were tempted to give you money (for graduate school, a car, a down payment on a house, etc.), but we knew that doing so might bring us joy in the short run, but would be detrimental to your growth in the long run. For this reason we made a conscious decision not to give you large cash gifts while we are alive.

It is statistically likely that one or both of us may live a long time. You could be near retirement age before you receive an inheritance. For those of you who didn't accumulate enough money for a comfortable retirement, we will be your ultimate safety net. Those of you who were more adept at accumulating wealth can pass your inheritance on to your children and grandchildren or give to charity.

While you are already mature adults, you might be surprised to learn we have left the money in trust for you. We want to explain our logic.

Trusts provide a number of valuable features.

- **Creditor Protection: We live in a litigious society and people with wealth are often sued. A trust will protect the assets for your benefit.**

· *Privacy: A trust provides a certain amount of protection from those who would prey on people coming into sudden wealth.*

· *Management: Comingling your assets, at least initially, will give you economies of scale. Furthermore, trustees are held to a "fiduciary" standard and must professionally manage the assets for your benefit.*

· *Insurance: A good portion of your inheritance will be life insurance proceeds. Having this owned by an irrevocable trust is particularly tax-efficient.*

· *Multi-Generational: For those of you who choose to pass all or a portion of your inheritance on to your children or grandchildren, these trusts allow you to do so without having to pay additional estate taxes.*

· *Flexibility: These trusts have been drafted to provide you both protection and the flexibility to meet your individual needs.*

Upon our deaths, a sizeable portion of our estate will be left to charity. Specifically, it will be left to our existing Donor Advised Fund at our local community foundation. We have given this considerable thought and our rationale is as follows:

· *We have been active in our community. During our careers, we have served on numerous non-profit boards, often serving in leadership positions. We believe in their missions. We gave to them while alive and intend to continue to support them after our deaths.*

· *It is our intention to let you begin to make small gifts out of our Donor Advised Fund now. We believe it builds good citizenship, lets us gain insight into what each of you is passionate about and creates a forum for us to interact as a family for a common purpose. If you show an interest and aptitude for giving money away effectively, we ultimately would like to have you direct some of the funds in our Donor Advised Fund after our deaths. We believe it could be an excellent way for you to meet annually as a family and teach your children the joy of giving.*

· *Under current tax law, charitable giving is tax-efficient. Incorporating philanthropy into our planning not only allows us to achieve the benefits above, but to pass our entire estate with little or no shrinkage due to income or estate tax.*

In conclusion, we hope this letter sheds light on what is important to us and why we have chosen to distribute our assets in the manner we have.

- *We value education as an opportunity to broaden our minds and add value to society.*

- *We believe in hard work, self-discipline and the self-esteem that comes from making it on your own.*

- *Through judicious use of trusts, we feel we have provided you both protection and flexibility.*

- *By providing you a predetermined amount of inheritance, we believe we have left a strong safety net, yet enough incentive to do your very best.*

- *We have purposefully delayed your inheritance to provide us maximum lifetime financial security and provide you the opportunity to make your own way in the world on your own terms.*

- *We believe in giving back to those less fortunate and to use shared philanthropy as a method to build stronger family ties.*

We realize our plan is not perfect. No doubt we have failed to anticipate certain actions or circumstances. Please accept the mistakes we may have made with the knowledge that we have done the best we can with the tools we have. The ultimate test of success will be if this plan allows you to reach your full potential and is not a detriment to your personal growth.

Living a life that matters doesn't happen by accident. It is not a matter of circumstance, but of choice. It is our sincere hope that you choose to live lives that matter and our estate plan will help you to achieve that end.

With love,
Mom & Dad

NEARY LETTER TO TRUSTEE

Mr. Jim Neary
111 South Street
Any City, Any State

Re: Trustee Duties

Dear Jim,

Thank you for agreeing to serve as trustee of our two irrevocable life insurance trusts (ILITs). You have been a great younger brother and I respect and trust your judgment. Know that we appreciate your commitment.

We don't mean for you to take this letter as a directive and it is certainly not legally binding. We are, however, trying to give you a cursory overview of your responsibilities as trustee and some insight into our hopes for our "legacy."

Each of our trusts is funded exclusively with a variable universal life insurance policy. The policy in the first trust is solely on my life. The policy in the second is a joint-life policy on the lives of both of us. The carrier is Massachusetts Mutual, a highly rated company. The cash values are currently invested exclusively in index funds with automatic rebalancing. Our intent is to stop making premium payments after John fully retires. Our agent, Allen Safe, will continue to administer the policies under your direction.

Your primary duties include, but are not limited to: administer the ILITs according to the trust documents, act solely in the interest and benefit of the beneficiaries, control and protect the trust property, act impartially, pay the premiums on a timely basis, manage the trust assets, send annual Crummey withdrawal notices to the beneficiaries, and keep the beneficiaries reasonably informed.

We have a team of trusted professional advisors (including Allen) with whom we have worked for years. They helped us to create our estate plan, our "Legacy Plan," and know how all the parts work together. It is our hope, barring some compelling reason, that you will continue to rely on them after our deaths. They can do virtually all of the administrative work for you. Your role is to exercise discretion and, in our place, sound judgment.

If, at any point in time, you are unable or unwilling to serve in this capacity, you certainly can resign. The trustees who would succeed you (in order) are: 1) Jane's sister, Monica and 2) U.S. National Bank. We never want these duties to become a burden or imposition on you.

As you know, we have always expected our children to work hard, be productive citizens and make their own way in the world. We have seen the detrimental effect that too much money (especially inherited money) can have on children/beneficiaries. That's why we have created a Legacy Plan and informed our children about our expectations.

Jane is the beneficiary of the trust with the policy insuring John's life. While we don't anticipate that Jane will need any money from this trust, if she requests distributions, I would expect you to be liberal in your discretion. We have been married for 40 years and completely trust each other's judgment.

Our three children (your favorite nieces and nephew!) are the beneficiaries of the trust that insures both our lives and are the ultimate beneficiaries of the trust that insures John's life. In choosing how and how much to leave an inheritance to our children, our primary purpose is to provide a "safety net." By that we mean that when they reach their retirement years, they can live comfortably.

Having said that, if our children do not have adequate resources of their own to cover normal expenses of health, education, maintenance and support, you certainly have our approval to make distributions to them as you deem necessary. We also give you our approval to allow them to withdraw up to the greater of $5,000 or five percent of their trust shares annually.

When each child reaches age 40, we have given each the opportunity to become the trustee of their own trust share. They simply need to put that request to you in writing, and receive your written permission. Unless there is an issue with creditors, predators, alcohol or chemical dependence, etc. we don't anticipate any reason why each child could not act as his/her own trustee. As they assume that role, you can resign and your trustee responsibilities will end.

As we write this letter, Jennifer, Nancy and Alex are responsible adults. Until we both die, there should be little for you to do. In the event we die earlier than we anticipate, we don't expect that our children will take any distributions from this trust until they reach age 40. At that time, they will likely become their own trustees. We have done all we can do to protect them and leave the rest to them. Thanks again for agreeing to serve as our trustee.

Gratefully,
John and Jane

THE VALUES WE HOPE TO PASS ON
JOHN & JANE NEARY

Our "legacy" is not simply the money we leave to non-profit organizations in our community. We believe that our greatest legacy is our children and the impact that they will have on making this world a better place to live. Through both example and the efforts we have made in the past and will make during our family meetings, we hope to pass on the following values:

Respect *We hope that our children first learn to respect themselves, then treat each person they meet with respect.*

Integrity *We want our children to always do "the right thing," especially when no one is looking.*

Hard Work *Hard work is a gift. It builds self-esteem and self-reliance.*

Modesty *Each of us is worth no more or no less than another in God's eyes. We are specks in the universe. Be humble.*

Frugality *We want our children to learn to live within their means. The satisfaction of buying material things is a fleeting pleasure.*

Generosity *We are blessed to have been born in this country and community and to have been part of a loving family. Help those less fortunate.*

Invitation To Children To Family Meetings
John & Jane Neary

Dear Jennifer, Nancy and Alex,

Recently, your mother officially retired from the University, and I announced my plan to sell my practice and phase into retirement over the next five years. Over the last year, your mother and I have spent time developing a Legacy Plan with the help of our professional advisors. We are anxious to share some of our plans with you.

An important part of our Legacy Plan involves holding annual family meetings to discuss financial matters. Specifically, we hope meetings will help us to:

1. Grow closer as a family.
2. Pass on our personal values through family stories and experiences.
3. Share with you what we have learned about managing personal finances.
4. Have fun!

We'd like to meet once each year for a half day at a time that is convenient for all of us. Each of you brings unique talents to our family and we are excited to establish this new family tradition.

Your mother and I will call you in the next few days to answer any questions you may have. In the meantime, start thinking about dates that you'd be able to meet.

Love,
Dad

INVITATION TO JOIN PERSONAL BOARD OF ADVISORS
JOHN & JANE NEARY

Dear Kathryn,

We write to invite you to become a member of the Personal Board of Advisors that we are forming to help us prepare for our retirement years. We are also inviting Curt (our attorney) and Allen (our financial advisor) to join our Board as you have all helped us in the past with professional advice. Rather than call on you on an as-needed basis, we'd like to expand our relationship. With this letter, you have our permission to share information freely with our other Board members.

The purpose of this Board is to help us maintain our financial security, modify our estate plan (if necessary) and develop a philanthropic plan. In addition, we expect you to collaborate with Curt and Allen and bring to us your best recommendations for the course of action that will help us reach our goals.

We would like to meet with our Board on a regular basis. We expect that to be several times during the first one or two years while we put our financial affairs in order. Thereafter, we'd like to meet annually.

The focus of each meeting will be our goals as they relate to our: financial security, estate plan and philanthropic giving. Occasionally, we may ask other advisors to join our meetings, but you three will be our source for comprehensive, coordinated advice.

We have asked Allen to be our Meeting Facilitator. He will schedule meetings (well in advance), work with us to set agendas, distribute any information you may need before or after meetings, take minutes and follow up on action items. We want these meetings to run like a typical board of directors meeting with each of you contributing your expertise and insights.

While we expect you to keep track of the time you spend preparing for and attending meetings (as well as performing any projects we authorize you to undertake during our meetings), we would like you to move from fee-for-service basis toward a retainer. We also ask that you name your own successor so we can expect uninterrupted service when you are not available either temporarily or permanently.

If you have any questions about what we are proposing here, please give us a call. We are happy to further discuss our thoughts.

Kathryn, thank you and we look forward to hearing from you.

Sincerely,

John and Jane Neary

POST-DEATH PHILANTHROPY PLAN
JOHN & JANE NEARY

MM/DD/YYYY

Dear Jennifer, Nancy and Alex,

In addition to the financial legacy we have left each of you to enhance your own financial security, we also intend to leave a financial legacy to our community. Since graduating from the State University, we have made this city our home. We have engaged in meaningful careers and raised you here. Its people have given us much and we intend to return the favor upon our passing.

Over the years, we have volunteered for a number of non-profit organizations. For some, we have served as directors. To all we have given our time, energy and money. We believe in their missions and efforts to make our community a better place. For these reasons, we intend to leave modest bequests to three organizations and a significant contribution to the State University as endowed scholarships in both the history and architecture departments.

When the second of the two of us dies, a portion of our assets will go to the Community Foundation (CF) in the Neary Family Donor Advised Fund. The exact amount of that donation will depend on when we die, how much we spend during our lifetimes and the return our investments earn. We have completed paperwork for the CF directing it in the disbursement of the funds. Until we die, we retain the right to change the organizations (and the allocation amounts) that will receive our assets.

At this time, we have directed the CF to allocate what we leave as follows:

66% as we designate, and
33% as each of the three of you designate

Our 2/3 portion is to be distributed:
10% Rotary International
10% All Saints Church
10% United Way

70% State University (half each to the departments of history and architecture)

We have asked CF to divide the remaining 33% of the fund (the portion you will direct) into three separate and equal donor advised funds: one in each of your names. You may make contributions from those funds to the charitable organizations that are important to you. Ideally, you will use those funds as a teaching tool for your own children.

We believe that through giving to others we enrich our own lives. We hope you will find giving to be as rewarding as we have.

Best wishes,
Mom and Dad

STATEMENT OF INTENT
NEARY FAMILY EDUCATION TRUST

This Statement of Intent is intended to provide guidance to the Trustee and Power Holder of the Neary Family Education Trust (the "Trust"). It is not meant to be a directive nor binding in any way on the Trustee. It is merely meant to serve as an indication of our intent regarding the management and distribution of the Trust assets.

1. What is this "Education Trust?"

This is money we have saved to help our grandchildren pay for their college education.

2. Why are we doing this?

We have been very fortunate in that we have earned more than we are likely to need for our retirement. We believe that in our country, education is the key to be able to achieve financial independence. The cost of a college education is getting out of reach of the average American. This is our gift to our grandchildren.

3. How much will there be in this trust?

Over the years, we have saved $1,000,000 in a separate account for the purpose of funding our grandchildren's education. With good fortune, it will continue to appreciate. We will pay the income taxes on the income earned by the assets. We are hopeful the growth rate of the fund will roughly approximate the inflation rate of college tuition.

4. How are the funds invested?

At this point, a professional money manager has invested the funds for us in a diversified portfolio of stocks and bonds.

5. What if some of our children have more children than others?

This is not a gift from us to our children. This is a gift from us to our grandchildren. Each grandchild is equally special to us. In our eyes, each grandchild will be treated "equally."

6. Does it make a difference which type of school a grandchild attends?

It is our intent that school should provide each grandchild the skills he or she needs to pursue a career that would allow that grandchild to support himself or herself and achieve financial independence. At the appropriate time and based on his or her capabilities and talents, we expect each grandchild (with help from his or her parents) to make a prudent choice among public or private college, junior college or trade school.

7. What if a grandchild elects not to attend college?

If a grandchild elects to not pursue further education after high school, then it is our belief that he or she will not need our financial help. We are firm believers that not every individual should attend college. However, there are numerous trade schools, metropolitan colleges, junior colleges, etc., that help a person to learn to support himself or herself. The purpose of this fund is purely to help those grandchildren pursuing education after high school to offset a portion of the associated costs. If a grandchild does not pursue education after high school, then that grandchild will not be eligible to receive funds from the Trust.

8. How much tuition assistance can a grandchild anticipate?

Our plans are based on the following assumptions:

- *Maximum tuition assistance provided per grandchild will not exceed the aggregate cost of four years of full-time enrollment at State University, including tuition, room and board, fees and incidentals. When we set up this trust this figure was $25,000 per year. This figure should be recalculated each year to adjust for inflation. We are not suggesting our grandchildren all must attend State University (although it could be a good choice!). We are merely using that cost as the guideline for the maximum we want the Trust to provide for each grandchild.*

- *Our funding assumes four years of schooling: 16 hours x 8 semesters = 128 hours.*

- *6% investment return (We are paying the income tax.)*

- *Ten grandchildren x $100,000 (4 years x $25,000) = $1,000,000.*

- *If there is more money than needed due to fewer than anticipated grandchildren, greater investment returns, etc., then the Trustee could use some of the excess funds to help pay for a portion of certain grandchildren's graduate school.*

9. What if a grandchild takes more than four years to graduate?

We are not guaranteeing to pay all of our grandchildren's college costs. We have set a fixed amount aside to help offset some of the costs of higher education. We do not intend to put additional money into this fund. When each grandchild graduates from high school, a fixed dollar amount (see above) may be "earmarked" for that child's education by the Trustee. Distributions may be less than that amount, but they will not exceed it.

Our intent is to create a strong incentive for each grandchild to continue his or her education then start a meaningful career. It should not reward dropping out, failing to make meaningful progress towards a degree or certification or unnecessarily prolonging one's education. The term "school" comes from a Greek word that means "free time." School was actually a reward or an honor that was bestowed upon a young person who didn't have to work in the fields a full day, but was allowed to spend some time thinking, learning and becoming exposed to new ideas. We anticipate the Trustee will allow each grandchild no more than six or seven years to complete a degree program. After that point, the Trust should no longer be a source of financing. We strongly encourage our grandchildren to work at least part-time to help pay for part of the cost of their schooling. It has been our experience that children make more prudent decisions when they are helping pay their own tuition.

10. What if a grandchild delays going to college?

There are good reasons some children don't go on to higher education upon completing high school. Some examples might be military service, volunteer work, internships, medical complications, etc. We believe everyone needs to work hard and make a meaningful contribution to society. For practical reasons, this fund cannot be an "open-ended" offer to reimburse educational costs. Unless there are extraordinary reasons, we anticipate any grandchild who does not begin an educational experience toward a degree or certificate program by the age of 25 will no longer have access to this fund. The amount "earmarked" for him or her can be held in the fund and used for future recipients.

11. What if one of our children marries someone who already has children?

We do not intend to make any further contributions to this fund. How much will be available will depend on many factors: investment results, taxation, tuition costs, the number of grandchildren, etc. We currently have ten grandchildren, and we think you're done? Dividing this fund too many ways could significantly reduce the amount available to any one recipient. With that in mind, it is our intention at this point in time not to include those children from previous or subsequent marriages unless they are adopted and raised by our child since a very young age and treated as their own. However, in order to retain flexibility, we have granted a Power Holder appointed under the Trust the ability to add as a beneficiary of the Trust any stepchild of one of our children, with the intent that it may become appropriate to include a stepchild who has been raised and treated as our child's own child. We realize this decision will be subjective, and the final decision must be made by the Power Holder considering all factors at that time, including our child's relationship with his/her stepchild, the number of our other grandchildren and available assets in the Trust.

12. What if a grandchild earns a "full ride?" Is he or she precluded from getting funds from the Trust?

Our intent is to allow all of our grandchildren, regardless of financial ability, to attend college, trade school or vocational school as a means to a meaningful career. We certainly don't want to create a disincentive for a highly motivated student. If a grandchild earns a full ride for undergraduate education, we would be fine if the Trustee would allow assistance with graduate school immediately following college, up to the amount originally "earmarked" for college, assuming there appears to be adequate funds available for other grandchildren.

13. Why did you choose a trust instead of more traditional 529 college savings vehicles?

We seriously considered using a 529 plan. It likely would have saved us hundreds of thousands of dollars in income taxes. However, we were willing to pay the additional income taxes for the flexibility and control of a trust.

In deciding to set aside money that we could have personally consumed in our retirement years, we want this Trust to reflect our values and be consistent with our estate planning documents.

1. *We do not believe our grandchildren are "entitled" to a college education paid for by their grandparents. Rather, we want them to have an "opportunity to earn" a college degree with the help of their grandparents.*

2. *We want our children involved in making decisions regarding their own children's education.*

3. *We want our children to work together as a cohesive unit for the benefit of the family's next generation.*

4. *We didn't want to preclude worthy grandchildren from earning scholarships or loans based on need or merit simply because they had a funded 529 plan.*

14. Will the Trustee make all final decisions when there is a dispute?

Yes. The Trustee has legal authority over the investments, administration and distribution of all Trust assets. However, it is our intent that our family will meet annually to discuss this Trust. We anticipate it will be a number of years until our first grandchild graduates from high school. We want our children to actively work together in planning for the distribution of these funds. It is our hope that the Trustee will solicit the input of all of our children and reach decisions by consensus. In those situations where a consensus cannot be reached, the Trustee's decision will be final.

15. How will the funds be disbursed?

The Trustee, with input from our children, will make decisions about how to disburse the funds. The Trustee may decide to pay funds directly to the institution, to the child or to the parent of the child for that child's benefit. Ideally, the grandchild (perhaps with his/her parents cosigning) will borrow all cost of tuition, room and board and fees for the first semester. After proving to the Trustee with documentation that he/she is making progress toward obtaining a degree or other certification in a particular educational endeavor, he/she will be able to submit those bills for reimbursement. That way, the grandchildren have some "skin in the game" and will realize that the Trustee only pays for performance and progress towards a degree or certification. It has been our experience that when children pay for a portion of their tuition or are "on the hook" for part of their education, they work harder and make more mature decisions. Under this approach, upon successfully graduating, a good portion (or all) of the cost of education will be fully reimbursed.

16. When will the fund end?

At this time, based on our assumptions, we should be able to provide a "full ride" to a four-year, in-state college for 10 grandchildren. Using reasonable assumptions, it could be as many as 30 years until the last grandchild graduates from college. The Trust directs the Trustee to terminate the Trust when the last grandchild reaches the age of 25. Presumably, there will be some money left in the Trust. Upon dissolution of the Trust, any remaining funds will be contributed to our donor-advised fund (The Neary Family Charitable Fund) at The Community Foundation.

Concluding remarks

We are pleased to be able to establish this fund for our grandchildren. After putting three children through private grade school and high school and then college, we are painfully aware of the financial burden of education. However, we feel it has been a wonderful gift from us to our children. It would have been much simpler for us to maintain ownership of these funds or establish traditional 529 plans.

Establishing an education Trust has been complex and expensive. However, we believe it is a testament to our trust and belief in our children. There will be complications and disagreement at times. However, by meeting annually and working together, we believe that we will grow stronger as a family. By forming the Trust now and sharing knowledge of its existence with our children, they can set realistic expectations for how much they and their children may have to contribute toward their children's education. Our ultimate hope is that our grandchildren will know that they can go to college if they work hard and our children will have the confidence they can afford it.

Dated this _____ day of _____, 20_____.

John Neary

Jane Neary

CHAPTER 8

Create Your Legacy

The purpose of life is not to be happy. It is to be useful,
to be honorable, to be compassionate, to have it make some
difference that you have lived and lived well.
RALPH WALDO EMERSON

Our country is in the midst of the largest transfer of wealth in its history. As a result of favorable legislative changes and sophisticated estate planning techniques, we are able to pass an increased percentage of our wealth to our children. Yet individuals and the professionals who advise them remain focused on the transfer of wealth with NO attention to what will happen to that wealth or to children who may be unprepared to handle it.

I have used this book to fill that gap and help individuals attach meaning to their wealth. "Legacy Planning" as I have described it incorporates:

1. Passing as much wealth as possible with minimal cost and taxation (traditional estate planning);

2. Passing personal values to our children;

3. Equipping our children to handle the money we leave wisely and in accordance with our values, and

4. Sharing our surplus with our communities.

In our society, you have the legal right to choose whomever you wish to receive your assets upon your death. Your choices impact those recipients, and the larger your estate, the greater potential for enormous benefit or damage to those recipients. Through Legacy Planning, you determine the type of impact your assets will have and expand, if you desire, the number of people you can affect.

I hope what I have written inspires you to go beyond simply handing off your wealth to your children and motivates you to make intentional decisions about how and to whom you will pass your wealth and values. There is simply too much at stake for your family and your community to make default or cookie-cutter decisions.

I have found that individuals who engage in Legacy Planning, share three characteristics: confidence in their financial security, a desire to pass on their values and a sense of gratitude for their success in life. With that in mind, my three goals in writing this book were:

1. Help you gain and maintain confidence that you can live your remaining years in a state of abundance rather than scarcity.

2. Show you how you can communicate your values to your children so that they will be better prepared to manage the inheritance you leave them in a manner that: a) aligns with your personal values and b) empowers them to be the best they can be.

3. Encourage you to express your gratitude for all you've received by sharing a portion of your surplus with organizations and causes that are meaningful to you.

Many ultra-wealthy families (think $100 million+) are already implementing parts or all of the Legacy Planning strategies I have shared with you here—typically through their family offices. I applaud their pioneering efforts and generosity.

But love of one's children and a desire to make a positive difference in this world are not the exclusive domain of the ultra-wealthy. Using the worksheets and forms in this book, I hope you will work with your existing trusted advisors to implement your own Legacy Plan.

"Legacy Planning" as I define it requires more than good intentions. It requires advisors willing to expand their idea of estate planning to encompass: passing values, including charitable giving and preparing heirs to receive assets. It requires you to be confident that your retirement years will be secure despite the occasional "What If?" questions that occur to you in the middle of the night. For those reasons

I recommend that you form and use a Personal Board of Advisors to help you gain that confidence and to create a personalized Legacy Plan. That Board should help you communicate your intentions and expectations to your children, and instruct your selected charitable organizations about how you'd like them to use the assets you leave in ways that are consistent with your values.

Unless you already work with the rare advisors who have incorporated Legacy Planning into their practices, you must take the initiative. If your advisors are not helping you to inject meaning into your legacy, give them a copy of this book. You must take charge to see that your estate plan is more than a tax-efficient transfer of assets. As I hope I have demonstrated, your legacy can be so much more!

I can't guarantee that creating a Legacy Plan will be easy. You may have to encourage, educate and empower your advisors and children. You will need both patience and persistence, but the result is well worth the effort. You will gain confidence in your financial security. You will tighten the bond with your children, play a role in their financial education and take comfort in their financial maturity. You will find joy in giving to causes and organization in your community about which you care deeply. You will enter your final years confident that you have left behind a meaningful legacy.

I wish you a successful journey to your desired spot on your Legacy Spectrum.

Mark A. Weber

Your Legacy Spectrum

I suggest that you jot down below the number of the paragraph you checked on each Legacy Spectrum. Total the numbers and divide by five.

Chapter	Spectrum	Paragraph Number
2	Financial Security	
3	Enough, But Not Too Much, For Your Children	
4	Legacy For Your Community	
5	Passing Your Values To Your Children	
6	Building A Personal Board Of Advisors	
	TOTAL:	
	Divide by 5:	

Where are you, currently, in the range of one to five? If you are not where you'd like to be in passing on your values, leaving a legacy and preparing your children, I suggest that you confer with your spouse and advisors. Use the techniques and worksheets that I've included in this book to move you toward the place you want to be on your personal Legacy Spectrum.

APPENDIX

Sample Worksheets & Letters

If you have decided to move beyond traditional estate planning and further along the Legacy Spectrum, I've included materials that may be helpful as you create your Legacy Plan. In this section you will find Sample Worksheets and Letters. Please use the following forms to craft your own Legacy Plan with input from your advisors. Together you can build a stronger family and community.

Sample Worksheets / Letters

Why We Choose to Leave Money To Our Children

Legacy Worksheet

How We Chose Our Inheritance Amount

How We Would Like Our Children To Use Their Inheritance

Legacy Plan Letter To Children

Letter To Trustee

Letter To Power Holder

The Values We Hope To Pass On

Invitation To Family Meetings

Invitation To Join Personal Board Of Advisors

Post-Death Philanthropy Plan

Educational Funding Letter

Assessment Of Prospective Members Of Your Personal Board Of Advisors

SAMPLE
WHY WE CHOOSE TO LEAVE MONEY TO OUR CHILDREN

Most estate planning presupposes that parents want to leave assets to their children upon their deaths. Leaving assets, however, is a choice. Under the law, you may leave your assets to any individual, institution, or entity you choose. If you do not have living children, or choose not to leave them assets upon your death(s), please so indicate below. If you have living children (and/ or grandchildren), however, and you intend to leave a portion of your estate to them, please articulate the three or four specific reasons you have chosen to do so. If you are married, it is important to complete this worksheet together.

❑ We do not have living children or do not want our assets to pass to them.

_____

_____

❑ We want to leave a portion of our wealth to our children for the following reasons. In order of priority those reasons include:

1. _____

_____

2. _____

_____

3. _____

_____

4. _____

_____

Note: This form has no legal binding effect. *Your advisors may use it to trigger thought, discussion and dialogue as they work to create a Legacy Plan for you.*

Name _____

Date: _____

SAMPLE
Legacy Worksheet

Before you and your spouse set an inheritance amount that is appropriate for your family, I suggest that you first ask yourselves several thought-provoking questions about your situation, your children and your current plan to transfer your wealth. Once you have reached a consensus, share your answers with your advisors. Doing so provides them valuable insight and guidance as they create your Legacy Plan.

Your Situation

What is your approximate net worth? _____

What is the nature of your assets (e.g. closely held business, farmland, commercial real estate, life insurance, securities)?

_____

How old are you? _____ and _____

What is your estimated life expectancy? _____ and _____

How would you describe your relationship with your children?

_____

_____

What type of lifestyle do you live? _____

_____

_____

Your Children

How old are your children? _____

_____

Are they all from the same marriage? _____

Are they single, married, divorced? _____

_____

What career paths have they taken? _____

_____

What type of lifestyle did your children grow up in? _____

_____

What level of financial maturity have they exhibited to date? ____

_____

How have they handled any significant cash gifts you have given?

_____

Are they savers or spenders?_____

_____

Do you meet with your children regularly? _____

_____

Distribution Plans

Do you intend to leave an equal amount to each child? _____

_____

If not, please explain why. _____

_____

Is it your intent to transfer significant assets to your children during your lifetimes or only upon your deaths?

_____

_____

A. If at death, will you give to them outright or in trust?

_____

B. If in trust, when will your children ultimately receive the assets?

_____

SAMPLE
How We Chose Our Inheritance Amount

Complete this form only after you have answered the questions on Why We Choose To Leave Money To Our Children and The Legacy Worksheets.

1. We believe that today, our combined estates will be worth about $_____ upon our deaths.

2. We would like to leave each of our children an amount of as much as $_____ upon our deaths.

You can express this number as a flat amount or as a percentage of your total estate if you prefer. You can include a "not to exceed" instruction to the amount. You can adjust the amount for inflation or state a set, unchanging amount. If you desire, you can state different amounts or percentages for different children or treat all children the same. Use the lines below to describe your intentions.

_____

_____

_____

3. We choose to leave this amount because:
Mark all statements that apply and provide explanations, if appropriate.

❑ The amount should be enough to achieve most or all of the items (listed on our How We Would Like Our Children To Use Their Inheritance Worksheet) that we'd like to provide for our children.

❑ We think that we will have enough left in our estate at our deaths to provide this amount without affecting our retirement income needs.

❑ We believe that this inheritance amount will not affect our ability to make the charitable bequests we desire.

❑ It is our understanding that we can leave this inheritance to our children without adverse tax consequences.

❑ We will develop (or have already developed) a plan to help educate our children on how to handle an inheritance of this size in accordance with our values.

❑ It is our understanding that we can use trusts (or other entities) to protect our children's inheritance from creditors and predators.

_____

_____

_____

_____

_____

_____

_____

Names _____

_____

Today's Date _____

*Note: While this form is designed to help you be purposeful in the distribution of your assets upon your death, **it has no legal, binding effect.** Your advisors will use it to initiate dialogue with you in the development of a Legacy Plan customized to meet your specific goals.*

SAMPLE

How We Would Like Our Children
To Use Their Inheritance

The purpose of this Worksheet is to help you make decisions about how you want your children to use the money you will leave and communicate your wishes to them. Both spouses should agree on the approximate amounts. While you cannot mandate how your children actually spend the money, this exercise will help you calculate an approximate amount that is comfortable for you. You may also use this Worksheet to clarify and communicate your values to your children at the appropriate time.

Check the items that reflect your intentions and add others as you desire. Use the blank lines to add your thoughts, comments or explanations.

We would feel good about our children using the inheritance they may receive from us to:

❑ Further their (or their children's) education.

_____

_____

_____

_____

Range: $ _____

❑ Pay off debt.

_____

_____

_____

_____

Range: $ _____

❑ Be able to retire at normal retirement age and live their final years self-sufficiently.

_____

_____

_____

_____

Range: $_____

❏ Purchase a bigger home.

_____

_____

_____

Range: $_____

❏ Start or acquire a business.

_____

_____

_____

Range: $_____

❏ Create an emergency fund.

_____

_____

_____

Range: $_____

❏ Purchase a vacation home.

_____

_____

_____

Range: $_____

❏ Start an investment fund.

_____

_____

_____

Range: $_____

❏ Collect art, jewelry, sports cars, etc.

_____

_____

_____

Range: $ _____

❏ Help those less fortunate through gifts to charity.

_____

_____

Range: $_____

❏ Other use

_____

_____

_____

Range: $_____

❏ Other use

_____

_____

_____

Range: $_____

Additional comments:

_____

_____

_____

_____

Names *(parents)*: _____

Date: _____

SAMPLE
Legacy Plan Letter To Children

MM/DD/YYYY

Dear Children:

We recently updated our estate planning documents. Although we are in excellent health and hope to live for many years to come, life is unpredictable. While our documents explain "how" our assets are to be distributed, this letter explains "why" we structured our estate plan in the manner we did.

Parents teach their children throughout their lifetimes by both their words and actions. Our estate planning and other documents will be our last "lesson." We want them to reflect our values.

This letter is not a legal document and does not supersede our will or trusts. Where there appears to be inconsistencies, the legal documents control. We write this merely as a means to explain our intent.

In "broad brush" terms, our estate plans leave our assets upon our deaths to each other. Only upon the death of the second spouse will assets pass to you. While you will each receive an equal share, it will be a specific dollar amount (with an inflation provision). The balance will pass to our charitable foundation.

While our parents met all of our needs as children, when we finished our schooling it was made clear we were on our own to make our way in the world. When we had our first child, your mother decided she wanted to stay at home until you all were in school. Since she had a good job and I had just started working, that choice put a financial strain on us. Business was quite slow in the early years and we had little discretionary income as our family grew. But we had each other. Our friends were in a similar situation and we had fun making do with the little we had. When our last child went off to school, your mother went back to work. Money was tight when you were young, but we have no regrets. We are very pleased with how each of you has turned out.

The primary goal of my estate plan is to make certain your mother has absolute financial security for the remainder of her life. Because

I have complete confidence in her judgment, my trust documents provide significant latitude to her while still being tax-efficient and providing protection from creditors and predators.

One of the wonderful gifts our parents gave each of us was a college education. We didn't have a true appreciation of this until we had multiple children in college at the same time. It was only then we realized the financial sacrifice our parents had made.

(If you have taken steps to finance your grandchildren's educations, consider the following explanation.)

While we helped you through college, we also want to help your children, our grandchildren. We have set aside a certain sum of money for our grandchildren's college tuition. We do not know how many will go to college or how much college will cost. We feel reasonably confident we have accumulated enough to pay four years of in-state tuition, plus room and board for each grandchild. Your children may take more than four years, may go to private or out-of-state schools. You will still need to save for their schooling. However, we are confident we have provided them a significant head start. (In a separate letter, we have spelled out in more detail our educational fund.)

Perhaps the greatest gift our parents left us was the example of hard work and living within their means. We were given the freedom to fail and the opportunity to make it on our own.

Over the years, we have witnessed the impact of inherited wealth on beneficiaries. Some children are able to handle the wealth wisely. We've found this particularly true if the inherited asset is a family-owned business. However, when the wealth is cash or securities, more often than not, the impact can be detrimental. The recipient often has low self-esteem and tends to over compensate by buying big homes, fancy cars, jewelry, and living an extravagant lifestyle.

On many occasions we were tempted to give you money (for graduate school, a car, a down payment on a house, etc.), but we knew that doing so might bring us joy in the short run, but would be detrimental to your growth in the long run. For this reason we made a conscious decision not to give you large cash gifts while we are alive.

It is statistically likely that one or both of us may live a long time.

You could be near retirement age before you receive an inheritance. For those of you who didn't accumulate enough money for a comfortable retirement, we will be your ultimate safety net. Those of you who were more adept at accumulating wealth can pass your inheritance on to your children and grandchildren or give to charity.

(If you have set up a trust, consider the following explanation.)

While you are already mature adults, you might be surprised to learn we have left the money in trust for you. We want to explain our logic.

Trusts provide a number of valuable features.

- **Creditor Protection:** We live in a litigious society and people with wealth are often sued. A trust will protect the assets for your benefit.

- **Privacy:** A trust provides a certain amount of protection from those who would prey on people coming into sudden wealth.

- **Management:** Comingling your assets, at least initially, will give you economies of scale. Furthermore, trustees are held to a "fiduciary" standard and must professionally manage the assets for your benefit.

- **Insurance:** A good portion of your inheritance will be life insurance proceeds. Having life insurance owned by an irrevocable trust is particularly tax-efficient.

- **Multi-Generational:** For those of you who choose to pass all or a portion of your inheritance to your children or grandchildren, these trusts allow you to do so without having to pay additional estate taxes.

- **Flexibility:** These trusts have been drafted to provide you both protection and the flexibility to meet your individual needs.

(If you have set up a donor advised fund or private foundation, consider the following explanation.)

Upon our deaths, a sizeable portion of our estate will be left to charity. Specifically, it will be left to our existing Donor Advised Fund at our local community foundation. We have given this considerable thought and our rationale is as follows:

· We have been active in our community. During our careers, we have served on numerous non-profit boards, often serving in leadership positions. We believe in their missions. We gave to them while alive and intend to continue to support them after our deaths.

· It is our intention to let you begin to make small gifts out of our Donor Advised Fund now. We believe it builds good citizenship, lets us gain insight into what each of you is passionate about and creates a forum for us to interact as a family for a common purpose. If you show an interest and aptitude for giving money away effectively, we ultimately would like to have you direct some of the funds in our Donor Advised Fund after our deaths. We believe it could be an excellent way for you to meet annually as a family and teach your children the joy of giving.

· Under current tax law, charitable giving is tax-efficient. Incorporating philanthropy into our planning not only allows us to achieve the benefits above, but to pass our entire estate with little or no shrinkage due to income or estate tax.

In conclusion, we hope this letter sheds light on what is important to us and why we have chosen to distribute our assets in the manner we have.

· We value education as an opportunity to broaden our minds and add value to society.

· We believe in hard work, self-discipline and the self-esteem that comes from making it on your own.

· Through judicious use of trusts, we feel we have provided you both protection and flexibility.

· By providing you a predetermined amount of inheritance, we believe we have left a strong safety net, yet enough incentive to do your very best.

· We have purposefully delayed your inheritance to provide us maximum lifetime financial security and provide you the opportunity to make your own way in the world on your own terms.

· We believe in giving back to those less fortunate and to use shared philanthropy as a method to build stronger family ties.

We realize our plan is not perfect. No doubt we have failed to anticipate certain actions or circumstances. Please accept the mistakes we may have made with the knowledge that we have done the best we can with the tools we have. The ultimate test of success will be if this plan allows you to reach your full potential and is not a detriment to your personal growth.

Living a life that matters doesn't happen by accident. It is not a matter of circumstance, but of choice. It is our sincere hope that you choose to live lives that matter and our Legacy Plan will help you to achieve that end.

With love,

Mom & Dad

SAMPLE
LETTER TO TRUSTEE

MM/DD/YYYY

Name of Trustee
Street Address
City, State ZIP

RE: Trustee Duties

Dear *(Name of Trustee)*:

Thank you for agreeing to serve as Trustee of our Irrevocable Life Insurance Trusts (ILITs). You are a great *(friend/sibling)*, and we respect and trust your judgment. Know that your commitment is appreciated.

This letter is not meant to be a directive and certainly is not legally binding. We are merely trying to give you a cursory overview of your responsibilities and some insight into how we might handle a situation.

Each trust is funded with a variable life insurance contract – one on my life and the other on both of our lives. The carrier is *(ACME Life,)* a highly rated carrier. The cash values are invested in index funds with automatic rebalancing. *(John Doe)*, agent, will continue to administer the policies under your direction.

Your primary duties include but are not limited to: administer the ILIT according to the trust document; act solely in the interest and for the benefit of the beneficiaries; control and protect the assets; act impartially; pay premiums on a timely basis; manage the trust assets; send annual Crummey withdrawal notices to the beneficiaries; and keep the beneficiaries reasonably informed.

We have a team of trusted professional advisors with whom we have worked for years. They are appraised of our complete estate plan, helped us to create our Legacy Plan, and know how the various parts work together. It is my hope, barring some compelling reason, that you would continue to use them. They can do virtually all of the administrative work for you. Your primary role is to exercise discretion and be our substitute in exercising sound judgment.

If at any point in time you are unable or unwilling to serve in this capacity, you certainly can resign. The line of trustee succession is: 1.you, 2. *(Successor Trustee Name)*, and 3. a corporate trustee. We never want our plan to be a burden or an imposition on you.

We expect our children to work hard, be productive citizens and make their own way in the world. We have seen the detrimental effect too much inherited money too early in life can have on beneficiaries.

In choosing how much and how to leave an inheritance to our children, our primary purpose is to provide a "safety net" so when our children get to their retirement years, they can live comfortably. Having said that, if our children do not have resources of their own for normal expenses of health, education, maintenance and support, you certainly have the discretion to make distributions as you deem necessary. They also may withdraw up to the greater of $5,000 or 5% of their trust share annually.

(Spouse's Name) is a beneficiary of my Irrevocable Trust. While we do not anticipate *(he/she)* will need any money from this trust, if *(he/she)* requests distributions, I would hope you would be liberal in your discretion. We have been married for over 40 years, and I completely trust *(his/her)* judgment.

As each child reaches age 40, they have the opportunity to become their own trustee. They simply need to submit a request to the Power Holder *(Name)* and receive his/her written permission. Unless there is an issue with creditors, predators, alcohol or chemical dependence, etc., we don't anticipate any problem with a child becoming his or her own trustee. At that point, you can resign and your trustee responsibilities will end.

At the time of this writing, all of our children have become responsible adults. Until we both die, there should be little for you to do. In the event we die earlier than anticipated, we don't expect that they will take distributions from this trust before they reach age 40. At that time, they will likely become their own trustees. We will have done all we can to protect them up until that time, and then it will be up to them.

Thank you again for agreeing to serve as our trustee.

Gratefully,

_____

Names of Trust Creators

SAMPLE
Letter To Power Holder

MM/DD/YYYY

Power Holder's Name
Street Address
City, State ZIP

Dear *Name of Power Holder*:

Thank you for agreeing to serve as a backup Trustee and Power Holder under my estate plan. I've watched you mature into a successful person, spouse, parent and involved citizen. I respect the person you've become and am confident you will exercise sound judgment on behalf of my family if called upon to do so.

In very broad terms, my estate plan leaves my assets to my *(wife/husband)* then equally to our children plus an amount to a charitable foundation. The amount our children will receive is capped at a specific amount. In addition, a separate trust has been established to provide a scholarship fund for our grandchildren's college education. Lastly, a significant amount will be left to our Donor Advised Fund at our community foundation, to be distributed pursuant to a written plan.

Upon my death, my *(wife/husband)* will become Trustee and Power Holder for *(his/her)* lifetime. You would only step in to serve in the event of my *(wife's/husband's)* death. At the time of this letter, we are age _____ and _____ and our children are ages _____. All of them have become mature, responsible adults who we feel are capable of handling money responsibly.

Under the terms of the trust, each child may become his or her own trustee with your written permission. In the unlikely event we both die before each child turns _____, they would need your permission to be their own trustee. It is my hope that you would grant such permission unless you are trying to protect assets from themselves or others. Circumstances that might cause you to deny a request to be their own trustee might be: bankruptcy, attachment by creditors, divorce, chemical dependency, incapacity, etc. In the highly unlikely event a child has completely disenfranchised himself or herself from the family, you have the authority to distribute their share to the other children or direct all or a portion of that child's proportional share to charity.

We have made it clear to our children that we expect them to work hard, contribute to society and make it on their own. We have little interest in giving them significant amounts of cash during our lifetimes. We will help them pay for education for their children. Most importantly, we will leave a financial safety net so when their working careers are over, they can retire with financial security. If there is more money than they reasonably need at that time, they will have the option to leave the remainder in trust for their heirs.

We have built a professional advisor team that is familiar with our overall Legacy Plan. Barring some compelling reason, I would anticipate you would continue to rely on them for advice and information. They can handle all of the administrative functions (tax returns, money management, correspondence, etc.) required of you. Your primary role is to understand our children's circumstances, work with them and exercise your judgment.

If there comes a time when you are unable or no longer desire to serve in this capacity, you can resign. The following order of succession is: *(1. Name, 2. Name, 3. Name)*, then a corporate trustee.

I believe it is likely either or both of us, will live to an old age. By that time, there will have been many changes and we will likely have made changes to our documents. Life is uncertain, and death can occur at any time. It comforts us to know that you are there as a "back stop" to carry out our financial plans for our children. Thank you.

Sincerely,

Name of creator of the trust

SAMPLE
The Values We Hope To Pass On

Our "legacy" is not simply the money we leave to non-profit organizations in our community. We believe that our greatest legacy is our children and the impact that they will have on making this world a better place to live. Through both example and the efforts we have made in the past and will make during our family meetings, we hope to pass on our values

Check five or six of the following values that are important to you and write your comments describing how you interpret each value and/or how you want your children to live them out.

Value	Your comments
_____	_____
	_____
_____	_____
	_____
_____	_____
	_____
_____	_____
	_____
_____	_____
	_____
_____	_____
	_____

Please see next page for a list of possible values.

Some examples:

VALUE	YOUR COMMENTS
Hard work	*Hard work is a gift. It builds self-esteem and self-reliance.*
Integrity	*We want our children to always "do the right thing," especially when no one is watching.*
Gratitude	*We have been given many blessings. We must be thankful through our words and actions.*
Modesty	*Each of us is equal in God's eyes. Be humble.*

Values

Abundance	Excellence	Kindness
Acceptance	Fairness	Knowledge
Accountability	Faith	Leadership
Achievement	Financial	Love
Appreciation	Independence	Loyalty
Commitment	Fitness	Modesty
Compassion	Frugality	Perseverance
Competence	Generosity	Pride
Contribution	Health	Respect
Courage	Honesty	Restraint
Dependability	Humility	Self-reliance
Discipline	Integrity	Self-respect
Education	Intelligence	Sharing
Empathy	Involvement	Success
Ethics	Justice	Trustworthiness

SAMPLE
Invitation To Children To Family Meetings

Use this letter as a template for one you will write to introduce your children to the concept of family meetings. Just as each family is unique, so too is each invitation. Yours should reflect your goals and your family.

MM/DD/YYYY

Dear Children,

Your *(mother/father)* and I have spent a good deal of time updating our estate and legacy plans. You are an essential part of our legacy and an essential part of the next phase of our planning.

In this phase, we intend to gather, once each year, as a family for two to three hours to discuss aspects of the legacy we wish to leave. We will chose a meeting time and place that is convenient for all of us.

Our goals in holding family meetings are:

1. Develop trusting relationships that can serve as a foundation from which to make difficult family decisions.

2. Pass on our values to you through sharing family stories and our experiences.

3. Discuss the goals we want our estate plan to accomplish

4. Help prepare you to handle a significant financial inheritance.

While there are some logistics to work out, your *(mother/father)* and I are excited to spend time with you and share this important part of our lives. We will call you in the next few days to answer your questions. In the meantime, think about some dates and times for our first meeting that would work well for you.

Love,

_____

(Mom / Dad)

SAMPLE
INVITATION TO JOIN PERSONAL BOARD OF ADVISORS

MM/DD/YYYY

Dear _____,

We write to invite you to become a member of the Personal Board of Advisors that we are forming to help us prepare for our retirement years. Specifically, we want you to help us maintain our financial security.

We are also inviting _____ *(our attorney)* and _____ *(our financial advisor)* to join our Board as you have all helped us in the past with professional advice. Rather than call you on an as-needed basis, we'd like to expand our relationship.

We would like to meet with our Board on a regular basis, at least once per year. With this letter, you have our permission to share information freely with our other Board members. We expect you to collaborate with them and bring to us your best recommendations for the course of action that will help us reach our goals.

The focus of each meeting will be our goals as they relate to our: financial security, estate plan and philanthropic giving. Occasionally, we may ask other advisors to join our meetings, but you three will be our source for comprehensive, coordinated advice.

At our first meeting we will discuss which one of you is best equipped to be our Meeting Facilitator. That person will assume responsibility for scheduling meetings (well in advance), working with us to set agendas, distributing necessary information, following up on action items, taking minutes and acting as our primary contact. We want these meetings to run like a typical board of directors meeting with each of you contributing your expertise and insights.

While we expect you to keep track of the time you spend preparing for and attending meetings (as well as performing any projects we authorize you to undertake during our meetings), we would like you to move from a fee-for-service basis toward a retainer. We also ask that you name your own successor so we can expect uninterrupted service when you are not available either temporarily or permanently.

If you have any questions about what we are proposing here, please give us a call. We are happy to further discuss our thoughts.

Thank you and we look forward to hearing from you.

Sincerely,

_____

SAMPLE
Post-Death Philanthropy Plan

MM/DD/YYYY

Dear Children,

As you know, your mother and I have left each of you a significant financial inheritance in our estate plan. It is our hope this will provide you financial security in your retirement years. Another part of our legacy is the ability to involve you in the distribution of funds we have earmarked for our community.

Currently, we have a charitable fund in place from which we make annual gifts. Specifically, it is a Donor Advised Fund ("DAF") at our local Community Foundation. We have been contributors for many years. It is a worthy organization in which we have a lot of confidence.

Upon our deaths, we have asked our Community Foundation to allow you to "step into our shoes" and make recommendations regarding the recipients' use of the funds. The purpose of this letter is to spell out our intentions.

While we could have simply made specific charitable bequests upon our deaths, we decided not to do that. Instead, we want to give you the opportunity to work together to make the final decisions. By allowing you to make the ultimate decisions, you can work as a family unit to learn from the organizations about their most pressing needs. You can compare their work to our values and make what you believe to be the decisions consistent with our family's values.

As of this writing, we have a significant amount in our DAF. We anticipate the amount will remain relatively level during our lifetimes. Whatever is left in our qualified retirement plans upon our deaths will be added to our DAF. Depending on investment performance and how long we live, this could be a sizable amount.

During our lifetime, we have been members of the "Heritage Society" of several nonprofits and committed to leave them funds upon our deaths. While not legally binding, we have given them our word. We anticipate you will honor our commitment. They are as follows:

$_____ *(name of organization)*
$_____ *(name of organization)*
$_____ *(name of organization)*

Consider whatever amount is left after these bequests in three separate "buckets."

Bucket 1: *Fifty percent* should be distributed within 36 months of the date of death of the survivor of us to the following organizations in our memories:

50%	ABC Charity
30%	DEF Charity
10%	GHI Charity
5%	JKL Charity
5%	MNO Charity

Rather than taking these percentages literally, use them as an indication of the percentages we would likely apply were we making the gifts today. You can decide if you wish to leave a gift to the organization's general, unrestricted fund or alternatively, you can decide if there is a certain project(s) you wish to support. You can make a single distribution or spread out the distributions so long as they are completed within the three years.

Bucket 2: *Twenty-five percent* should be distributed within 20 years of the date of death of the survivor of us. It can be done in equal annual payments or in chunks, as you determine. We would like you to work together, with input from our Community Foundation, and distribute the funds as you deem appropriate within the following parameters:

· The organization must be located in Our City and the funds spent in the Our City's area.

· The gifts should be consistent with our values and life's work. For example: We value: health, religion, education and development of leadership and good citizenship within youth.

· The distributions can be made anonymously or in the name of the fund. You can decide what you feel works best.

Bucket 3: *Twenty-five percent* should be segregated into as many donor advised funds (at our Community Foundation or in a donor advised fund you designate so long as it is approved by our Community Foundation) as there are of you who survive us and want to participate. Each child can have total freedom (within the legal restrictions of a donor advised fund) to distribute the funds to charities of your choice. You are free to, and we encourage you to, use donor advised funds as a teaching tool with your own children. We believe being able to give away money to help others less fortunate is an honor and can bring as much joy to the giver as the recipient. If at any time you feel this is a burden, please simply resign and let those siblings who derive joy and meaning from the process take your place.

We have intentionally set "sunset" provisions to provide you a sense of urgency and to make each distribution more significant.

If this plan is executed as we intend, we hope we will have accomplished the following:

· Given back to our community through organizations that have been important to us.

· Provided you an opportunity to meet in person annually (hopefully in Our City) to fulfill this "obligation" and grow closer as you work together for a common cause.

· Passed on some of our values and helped you identify those values we share as a family.

· Shared with you both the joy and responsibility of helping others.

Thank you for your thoughtful attention to helping us fulfill our Legacy Plan. It is an expression of our gratitude to our community as well as our faith and trust in you. Best of luck.

Love,

_____

(Mom and Dad)

SAMPLE

EDUCATIONAL FUNDING LETTER

Many grandparents wish to help their grandchildren with the cost of attending college. Some grandparents wait until their grandchildren attend college, and help fund the related costs from their current cash flow. Others give money to their children, and let them deal with their children's tuition costs. Others partially pre-fund college costs using tax-favored college savings vehicles such as 529 plans. Professional advisors can help you determine which funding vehicle best suits your particular circumstances, goals and current tax law.

This letter is an example of one you would write if you decided to pre-fund college costs using a 529 plan.

Dear _____,
      (children)

As you know, we are strong believers in the value of education. It is the foundation for good citizenship and the doorway to meaningful career opportunities.

Unfortunately, the cost of education in our country continues to rise at a seemingly unsustainable rate. Many students incur student loan debt that takes many years to pay off. We would like to help you save for the cost of your children's educations.

We plan to save up to $14,000 per year for each of our grandchildren as long as our cash flow permits. We will establish a 529 plan for each child. We will own the 529 accounts while we are alive. Upon our deaths, you, the parents, will become the owners of your child's 529 account. Each account may end up with different amounts depending on the child's age when we start funding the account, investment results and when funds are withdrawn for tuition. At this time, our intent is to discontinue our contributions to these accounts when we retire and begin living on less income.

Whether our grandchildren attend a university, community college or trade school makes no difference to us. Our hope is that each advances their learning so that they might pursue fulfilling careers.

Through our financial contributions, scholarships and their part-time jobs, we hope our grandchildren will be able to avoid significant debt as they complete their educations. If a grandchild decides not to pursue further education after high school, we envision that the balance of his/her 529 Plan will be rolled into the accounts of his/her siblings who pursue higher education.

It is our plan to review the investment earnings and plan balances each year at our Family Meetings.

With love,

_____

(Mom and Dad)

ASSESSMENT OF PROSPECTIVE MEMBERS
OF YOUR PERSONAL BOARD OF ADVISORS

Use the following scale to grade candidates:
  0: Don't know
  1: Strongly Disagree
  2: Disagree
  3: Agree
  4: Strongly Agree

QUALITY	CHARACTERISTIC	GRADE
Technical Competency	Advisor is technically competent in the area in which I require expertise.	0 1 2 3 4
Personal Concern	Advisor expresses genuine concern for me and my opinions through active listening.	0 1 2 3 4
Creativity	Advisor is proactive in suggesting both items for me to consider and possible solutions.	0 1 2 3 4
Timeliness	Advisor is timely in their responses to my calls and email messages.	0 1 2 3 4
Cooperation	Advisor listens to, speaks favorably of, and works well with other advisors.	0 1 2 3 4
Organizational Skills	Advisor is organized and prepared for meetings.	0 1 2 3 4
Successor Designate	Advisor has named a successor who could work, if necessary, with my surviving spouse and children.	0 1 2 3 4
Billing Practices	Advisor's billing practices are transparent and reasonable. Advisor is open to an annual retainer.	0 1 2 3 4

Resources

If you would like to learn more about the topics I've discussed in this book, I've found the following books to be particularly helpful.

Buford, Bob, *Halftime: Moving From Success to Significance*

Collier, Charles W., *Wealth In Families*

Fithian, Scott and Fithian, Todd, *The Right Side of the Table: Where Do You Sit In The Minds Of The Affluent?*

Gallo, Ph.D. Eileen and J. Gallo, Jon J., *Silver Spoon Kids: How Successful Parents Raise Responsible Children*

Gary, Tracy, *Inspired Philanthropy: Your Step-By-Step Guide to Creating a Giving Plan And Leaving A Legacy*

Grubman, Ph.D., James, *Strangers in Paradise: How Families Adapt To Wealth Across Generations*

Hausner, Ph.D., Lee, *Children of Paradise: Successful Parenting For Prosperous Families*

Hughes, Jr., James E., *Family Wealth: Keeping It In The Family: How Family Members and Their Advisers Preserve Human, Intellectual, and Financial Assets For Generations*

Santi, Jenny, *The Giving Way To Happiness: Stories and Science Behind The Life-Changing Power of Giving*

Stovall, Jim *The Ultimate Gift* (a novel)

York, David R., and Howell, Andrew L., *Entrusted: Building A Legacy That Lasts*

JUST FOR ADVISORS

JUST FOR ADVISORS

I wrote this book primarily for high-net-worth individuals. Our role as professional advisors, whether we act as "hired hands" or "trusted advisors" is to help them achieve their goals. In the context of estate and financial planning, that means helping them grow, preserve and transfer their wealth in a tax-efficient manner. We provide information and advice; our clients make the ultimate decisions.

The premise of this book is that estate and financial planning, as traditionally understood and practiced, is just one point on a continuum (or spectrum). Most of us, individuals and advisors alike, stop somewhere in the middle, not intentionally, but because we don't realize that there's more we can do to achieve financial and estate planning goals.

As planners, we often define "success" differently than our clients do. For example, as financial planners we typically view success as helping our clients accumulate enough money to support themselves through their retirement years. As estate planners, we are successful if we help our clients transfer their assets upon their deaths to the next generation with a minimum of taxation and expense.

Parents want the best for their children. They want them to live happy, fulfilling lives. They want the inheritance they leave to help, not hinder, their children as they pursue fulfilling lives. As advisors, however, we see our roles end once we've put in place the wealth transfer mechanism. Beyond that, we leave it to children to figure out how to manage and use inherited wealth. One author compared this handoff to a father who hands his 15-year-old son a loaded gun. If this father trains his son in its use, and regularly takes him hunting, this gift is an opportunity for spending quality time together and a shared love of a sport. Without training, instruction or the father's time, this gift could have horrific consequences.

I believe we can do better. We can look at how our clients define success and stretch ourselves to meet that definition. Over years of working with high-net-worth couples, I've learned that success only begins with passing assets to children with minimum taxation. To them, success means passing the "right" amount of assets, for the "right" reasons and in way that improves the chances for the "right" outcome. Yes, "right" varies by individual and by family, but in general, parents see their legacies as more than financial and success involves more than money.

How do we help our clients to move along the spectrum to leave the legacies they desire? We need to expand our own horizons with knowledge that isn't (currently) taught in our law or business schools, or in the financial services field. Yes, there are professional advisors who provide "legacy planning" services to the ultra-affluent. These advisors are well equipped to service those individuals who realize that real success involves more than accumulating assets and passing more of them on. These individuals seek to leave meaningful legacies and define success as:

1. Maintaining a sense of abundance during the last third of their lives;

2. Growing closer as a family through enhanced communication;

3. Teaching their children to be good citizens and wise stewards of their wealth; and

4. Creating meaning in their lives by giving their communities both their time and treasure.

I believe that this type of Legacy Planning need not remain the exclusive domain of the ultra-affluent who can afford national boutique planning firms. My hope in writing this book is to enable a broader group of individuals to access these services and equip practitioners to deliver these services to their clients.

There is a growing body of literature in this field for those willing to teach themselves. The Chartered Advisor in Philanthropy® (CAP®) program through The American College of Financial Services provides a wealth of resources and a structured learning environment. Creating the expertise within your firm or teaming up with other advisors with proven expertise are viable alternatives to expanding your ability to deliver legacy services to your clients on your own.

Numerous studies consistently show that high-net-worth individuals want and expect more from estate and financial planning.

I encourage you to consider incorporating legacy planning into your own practice.

In the pages that follow, I have described the many ways in which "traditional" planners differ from what I refer to as "legacy planners." It will become clear that I see legacy planners as offering numerous advantages to their clients and their children.

While I have had the unique opportunity to work with many affluent clients I acknowledge there are other planners who are brighter and more articulate than me. My goal was to create a springboard from which you might expand on and improve Legacy Planning. I urge you to collaborate with advisors in your communities to help your clients expand their legacy horizons.

In return, you will be rewarded with "deeper relationships with your clients," greater likelihood that your firm will retain the next generation as clients, more fun playing on a team of advisors, a steadier, more reliable stream of income and the satisfaction of knowing that you are doing your part to strengthen the fabric of families and your community.

ATTITUDES OF TRADITIONAL ESTATE PLANNERS
vs.
ATTITUDES OF LEGACY PLANNERS

Time and Fees

Traditional Estate Planner

"Client wants to get this done now and then not deal with it again for several years or more. Client will only pay me for two to three meetings."

Legacy Planner

"The client wants both documents that will carry out his or her intentions and help develop a comprehensive plan with ongoing maintenance. While fees must be within reason and communicated in advance, the client is willing to pay them."

Financial Independence

Traditional Estate Planner

"Client knows how much he or she spends and how much will be needed for a secure retirement. I don't need to deal with this issue."

Legacy Planner

"Before the client will be willing to part with any assets to reduce potential transfer taxes, he or she must be completely comfortable that he or she has enough assets to provide lifetime security. We will help him or her achieve this confidence through education and regular monitoring. By identifying and insuring against potential risks that could undermine the client's sense of security, we will provide assurance that he or she will always have enough. We will provide reassurance through regular meetings with the client, as well as with children if requested."

Children's Inheritance

Traditional Estate Planner

"The client will want to leave everything he or she can to the children and not pay any taxes. The children should receive their inheritance in pre-determined time intervals such as 25, 30 and 35."

Legacy Planner
"Parents want the best for their children. Some feel money reflects the amount of love they have for their children. Others feel money can be a detriment to their children's happiness. We will delve deeply in this area through a series of questions and by sharing experience with other clients help this client clearly think through this important issue. We will arrive at an answer that both spouses are completely comfortable with. Only when we have a firm commitment to the amount they desire to leave their children will we begin to develop a specific plan. This plan will be unique to this particular client. If the client is concerned about his or her children's maturity to responsibly handle a significant inheritance, we will help prepare the children to do so."

Philanthropy

Traditional Estate Planner
"The client probably won't want to leave any money to charity. If he or she does, it should be a testamentary bequest of all or a portion of whatever is left in the client's IRA."

Legacy Planner
"Every client has a set of values they feel strongly about and would like to see perpetuated through their children and in the community. We will help them discover their values through open-ended questions and active listening. After we have heard the client's story, helped the client achieve financial security, and come to peace with the children's inheritance question, we will introduce him or her to how giving back to the community may help further his or her values. Any giving recommendations will be in concert with the rest of his planning."

Additional Meetings

Traditional Estate Planner
"Once the documents are signed the client will not need me and will not be willing to pay me to meet with children or other advisors."

Legacy Planner
"In order to fully implement the client's plan, confirm goals have not

changed, adjust to changing circumstances and provide the client confidence in his or her planning, we will meet at least annually with the client's entire advisor team. While each advisor will need to charge for his or her time, the client will understand this is a small price to pay for the maintenance of the plan and the peace of mind it brings. Each advisor is important to the success of the client's plan, and will be kept appraised of all major developments."

Contrasting Advisors Involved
In Traditional Estate Planning
to
Legacy Planning

Traditional Estate Planner	Legacy Planner
CORE ADVISOR:	
Attorney	*Attorney, accountant, life insurance professional, money manager*
VIRTUAL ADVISOR:	
Life insurance agent, accountant	*Planned giving consultant, property and casualty agent, trustee*
PLAN REVIEW:	
Attorney reviews estate planning documents every three to four years or when client calls.	*Core advisors meet as a team one to two times each year with client and spouse.*

Advantages of Legacy Planning

To Clients

- Instills lasting confidence in having "enough."

- Crystallizes intentions regarding children's inheritance.

- Passes wealth tax-efficiently.

- Passes values to heirs.

- Enhances understanding and teamwork among family members.

- Protects wealth and promotes goals through ongoing involvement of Personal Board of Advisors.

To Clients' Children

- Provides comfort in knowledge that parents' financial affairs are in order.

- Provides opportunity for communication with both parents and siblings regarding finances and philanthropy.

To Professional Advisors

- Establishes foundation for ongoing, deep relationship with clients.

- Provides opportunity to work collaboratively with other advisors to benefit clients.

- Increases odds of acting as professional advisor to clients' heirs.

- Generates ongoing flow of predictable income.

- Achieves "traditional" goal of minimizing clients' taxes and "non-traditional" goal of giving back to community.

- Builds stronger families and minimizes potential for conflict.

Chartered Advisor In Philanthropy®
AND
CAP® Study Groups

William B. Wallace is the former CEO of Home Life Insurance Company and the former Chairman of the Board of The American College of Financial Services. In 1999, Bill and his wife, Sallie, established the Sallie B. and William B. Wallace Chair in Philanthropy at The American College of Financial Services. Through the Wallace Chair, The American College established the Chartered Advisor in Philanthropy® (CAP®) designation. The program is offered at the graduate level and as part of the College's Master of Science in Financial Services program. Philip Cubeta, CLU®, CHFC®, MSFS, CAP® is the current holder of the Wallace Chair.

In establishing the Chair in Philanthropy, the Wallaces had four primary goals:

1. Create awareness nationally of the need for philanthropic advisors;

2. Provide a comprehensive common curriculum for fundraisers and advisors;

3. Promote understanding of common issues for fundraisers and advisors; and

4. Help fundraisers and advisors understand each other's perspectives.

Individuals can earn the CAP® designation by taking on-line and self-study courses. Some, however, have studied the CAP® curriculum in groups, taking an inter-disciplinary approach to master the materials and earn the CAP® designation.

The first CAP® Study Group was formed in Dallas in 2009 to encourage this interdisciplinary approach among professionals. As of this writing, there are over 20 CAP® Study Groups throughout the U.S.

Omaha has been home to a CAP® Study Group each year since 2012 through its local community foundation. That program has produced, on average, 14 CAP® designees each year. In 2017, in an attempt to measure the impact that the Omaha CAP® program has had on the community, a confidential survey was conducted. Fifty CAP® program graduates (attorneys, accountants and financial service professionals) were asked to estimate how much wealth their clients had committed to charity since the advisor had used techniques and ideas learned in the CAP® Program. The eighty-six percent who responded estimated cumulatively that their clients had made current and future charitable gifts of $1.4 billion! They are truly having an impact on their communities!

CAP® Study Groups are an ideal environment in which professional advisors learn to collaborate to better serve both their clients and the communities in which they live.

I suggest that you contact The American College of Financial Services to see of there is an active Study Group in your area.

ACKNOWLEDGEMENTS

Acknowledgements

Writing one's first book is a daunting undertaking and truly a team effort. I want to acknowledge some members of my team here.

Professor Philip Cubeta, the face and voice of the Chartered Advisor in Philanthropy designation at The American College of Financial Services, encouraged me to write this book. Without his inspiration and kind words, this book would have remained just an idea.

The number of entrepreneurs and business leaders who have shared openly with our CAP® classes over the last five years has surpassed my wildest expectations. None was more important than Mike Yanney, CEO Emeritus and Walter Scott, Chairman and CEO Emeritus. Their legacies of generosity and leadership in the Omaha business community will be felt for generations.

Always a student, I constantly learn from my clients, speakers in the CAP® Study Group and the authors of the CAP® materials. Admiration and respect describe my feelings for the 60-something students who have successfully completed the Omaha CAP® Study Group Program. They are the best and brightest in the fields of law, accounting, financial services and planned giving. It is exciting to witness the impact they have already had, and will continue to have, in preparing heirs and promoting philanthropy in our community over the decades to come.

With great pride I have been a part of Silverstone Group for nearly 30 years and have watched it grow from a local risk-management consulting firm to a regional juggernaut with a national presence. My fellow associates (now nearly 250) have worked hard to earn the respect of Silverstone's clients and community.

The Omaha Community Foundation has been an incredible partner in hosting the Omaha CAP® Study Group Program. It is the philanthropic leader in Omaha and rated one of the top community foundations in the country. The unwavering support of Sara Boyd, CEO/President and Matt Darling, Vice President, has made every hour spent in leading the Program enjoyable.

It was Warren Buffett's words that inspired me to start Omaha's CAP® Study Group Program. He has inspired innumerable others through his words and actions in our city and beyond. He is known worldwide for being one of the wealthiest men on the planet. Arguably, he is the most charitable man on earth. In Omaha his quiet, modest generosity has spawned a culture of raising responsible children and giving to those less fortunate. The spirit of philanthropy runs deep in Omaha in no small part due to the "Buffett Effect."

I want to acknowledge Ron Quinn, a man most comfortable out of the limelight, for his early and continued support of the Omaha CAP® Study Group project. He believed in my vision, completed all of the CAP® coursework and has continued to be a vocal supporter and quiet contributor to the Program's success. In his personal planning he would score well on the Legacy Spectrum.

Bill and Sallie Wallace had the foresight and financial resources to endow the Chair in Philanthropy at The American College of Financial Services that gave birth to the Chartered Advisor in Philanthropy program. CAP®, in turn has trained over 1600 advisors to expand their thinking and help individuals expand, and make more meaningful their own financial legacies.

Writing this book without the help of my editor, Kathryn Bolinske, would not have been nearly as much fun. She navigated the shoals of writing, rewriting and publishing. Her insight, experience and advice were invaluable. Her energy and constant encouragement were indispensible.

My wife Tricia steadfastly supported me through this process despite the innumerable weekends and evenings I spent alone, sequestered in my home office. Thank you for your unfaltering love and encouragement.

There are many contributors to the literature of helping individuals prepare their children to receive financial inheritances, find joy in giving and better utilize the skills of professional advisors. While I have not met these individuals, I respect their scholarship and incorporate many of their ideas in my thinking. Some of the most notable include: Scott and Todd Fithian, David Holaday, Charles Collier, Bob Buford, Jim Collins, James E. Hughes, Jr. and Jim Stovall.

Estate planning attorneys are at the forefront of the estate/legacy planning experience. For 30 years I have been privileged to work with, and call friends, some of the very finest in my community and nationwide. I know that they are often under-valued for the work they do, and I hope Legacy Planning deepens their relationships with their clients and contributes to their roles as trusted advisors.

Finally, I want to thank the many families I have had the honor of working with over the years. They live the precepts of this book and have used their wealth to empower their children to become better citizens. In doing so, they have enriched our communities with their leadership, example and generosity.